Living
Waters

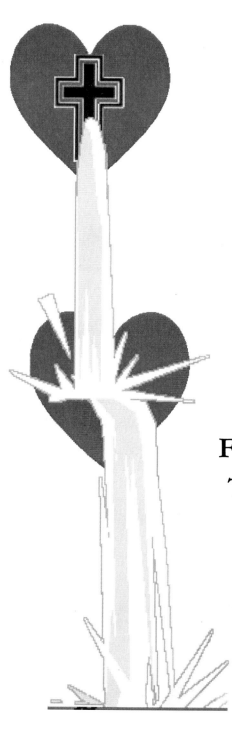

Baptism:

From His Heart
Through Ours

James
Lindemann

James (Jim) Lindemann

Webpage: lindespirit.com
email: jim@lindespirit.com
Blog: CovenantMusings.lindespirit.com

Other titles by the author:
COVENANT: The Blood Is The Life
Creation's Ballet for Jesus
Celebration! - Holy Communion: A Love Story
In the Image of God: Male and Female He Created Them
The Mystery of Suffering: Escape From or Presence Within Suffering

RFL & Son, Publisher
541 33 Street South
Lethbridge, Alberta, Canada T1J 3V7

RFL & Son, Publisher

ISBN 978-0-9916866-3-6
9 780991 686636
90000

Flyleaf

Baptism. Simple yet powerful and far-reaching. Indeed, it overflows with a range of blessings within a new relationship with the Creator of the universe. We receive Grace and Mercy, and God's Glory; we have His seal and "earnest" to confirm His promises, and are authorized to be Jehovah's "Image" – His representatives – to this cosmos. We are adopted as children in God's Family, made members within Christ's Body, placed into His Bride (the Church), become citizens of His Kingdom, and are His priests to His Creation. We are born again, become new creations, are raised to be temples of the Holy Spirit, and bear the fruit of the Spirit. We are valued for the individuals we are and have our place as our Lord does His work through us in our world. This relationship is from God's heart; He yearns to have this with all humans, from infant to the aged. All we do is to apply "the Water with the Word" in faith. And it is enough.

This is a close look at the astonishing range of blessings found within Baptism, arranged in a dual format: the first section is a very condensed overview of what God causes to occur within this simple act; the second section dives into the greatness of the promises and of the relationship that God has so desired with humans since Creation.

The Author

The author, a pastor himself, is the recipient of perspectives, concerns and interests handed down from a long line of pastors in the Lutheran Church, hence his interest and background in such things as the Sacraments, the Covenant, and even the Star of Bethlehem. His Bible Study groups have also contributed greatly in developing these various themes, and now as retirement approaches, this is a good time to gather these thoughts into a more finished form.

Born and raised in New York City, he has come to also value the life in the smaller communities. With his deeply appreciated companion (his wife), their family bulges at the seams with four natural, two adopted, a variety of foster children, and now grandchildren – there is no end to the usually delightful competition for his attention. Perhaps in the coming years there may even be time to pursue his Master's interest in carpentry.

Table of Contents

II. Baptism in Depth

Preface

A Sunday School teacher wanted something on Baptism which she could share with her students' parents and asked if I might put together some sort of an explanation. It turned out to be a more ambitious project than first expected. The problem is that Baptism is an enormous gift very full of God's grace and has many elements to it. The dilemma this creates is that on the one hand, describing the depth of the power and the majesty of this Sacrament can easily overwhelm and confuse a novice; yet on the other hand, simply touching on the highlights can give the impression of clichés and opinions which have no grounding other than romantic imagination.

The design of this book attempts to address both sets of needs. The first section gives a mosaic of the highlights – the important themes and concepts which are packed into this Sacrament; the second section spends more time dealing with the backgrounds to these concepts, identifying sources and reasonings behind them. This way one can have an overview of the Sacrament, and yet have available a deeper pursuit of the material.

Hopefully such a format would help when introducing Baptism's wonderful abundance of grace to someone not familiar with its full range, yet it can address the questions of those who wish to explore in more depth the Biblical sources to this doctrine.

I thank Jane Pollock for her proofreading. It seems that this time the manuscript was in dire need of her sharp eye and she has been willing to spend the time – and the encouragement – as she worked her expertise.

Jim Lindemann

November, 2014

Postscript:

Likely with varying degrees of accuracy, the Bible quote translations are mine, however there is a heavy dependence on:

The Interlinear Hebrew/Greek English Bible, 4 volumes
Jay Green, ed., (Lafayette, IN: Associated Publishers and Authors, 1979)

As well as
The Online Bible computer program (http://www.onlinebible.net)
Copyright in Canada
by Larry Pierce
(11 Holmwood St., Winterbourne, Ontario, N0B 2V0)

and particularly its modules for

The Authorized or King James (1769) Version

American King James Version
Michael Peter (Stone) Engelbrite (True Grace Ministries)
Placed into the public domain on November 8, 1999.

also its dictionary linking to *Strong's Concordance* numbers and to

R Laird Harris, *Theological Wordbook of the Old Testament* (Chicago: Moody Press, 1981)

Gerhard Kittel and Gerhard Friedrich, ed., *Theological Dictionary of the New Testament*, (Grand Rapids, MI: Wm. B. Eerdmans Publishing Co., 1966).

In addition to the website: *http://interlinearbible.org*

I.

Baptism in Overview

1. *Jehovah's Dream* (See pages 41-56)

The Context of Baptism

There are many misconceptions and misunderstandings about Baptism. To some it is just a word, for example "Baptism by fire" which speaks of a difficult initiation into something. Others see it as merely a ritual, "because you are supposed to do it." Some think of it as a sort of magical mystery, an automatic ticket to heaven, instant salvation – "just add water." And there are those who see it merely as a human activity, "I declare my faith." What is missed is that there is a long history which stretches all the way back to the first chapter of Genesis, which gives content to this Sacrament.

God's Design: Covenant – Backbone to the Bible

God deliberately creates the Universe so that He will be invisible. However, His plan is that a special creature will be the place where Creation can catch a glimpse of Him, something that will be in His "Image," something that will reveal His very Soul. That creature is man, but to be equipped for this task, the connection between the Creator and His creature must have to be intimate, personal and loving.

This is where "Blood" comes in: the Bible describes it as identical to, and the vehicle of, "Life" and "Soul" in Leviticus and Deuteronomy. The Hebrew word for "*likeness*" in Genesis 1:26 ("in Our likeness") is derived from "Blood," as are both the word for the "*ground*" and the word for the "*man*" who is formed from it [Genesis 2:7]. As well, no other creature is ever described as having the Breath of God blown into his nostrils.

The relationship by "Blood" ("Life," "Soul") is the basis of what would be called "Covenant" ("*Blood*-Covenant" - basically identical to the North American

"Blood-Brother" ritual), a relationship where the participants would cut their hands or arms and join the cuts to mingle the Bloods, thereby "becoming one Blood" and now one Life, one Soul, undivided, would "flow" between them. Powered by strong Love, as defined in Jonathan and David's Covenant [I Samuel 18:1-3] and reflecting Steadfast Love, it echoes the foundational bond with Himself in which the Creator places His new creature.

So deliberately essential would be this creature, that Jehovah (His Covenant Name) will not "take over" should man neglect his responsibilities. Things like feeding the hungry and clothing the naked will not even be done by the angels if humans despise being God's "'Soul'-likeness" (or "'Blood'-likeness"). Despite mankind's fall into rebellion, the Creator will not reconsider His partnership with this creature – He is that earnest about the role and the honor which humans are to have in His Creation.

In this "'Soul'-likeness," man is to reveal to the *cosmos* (the Greek word for "world") the Glory of God, which He Himself described in Exodus 33 and 34 as His goodness, Covenant relationship, grace, mercy, Steadfast Love, faithfulness, forgiveness and justice.

The Grace of the Circumcision Covenant

The bond in the Old Testament focus is the Circumcision Covenant. Even today the modern Jew looks to Circumcision as *the* mark of their identity as a People, as God's special People. Unfortunately though, by the time of Jesus this bond has acquired a lot of baggage and has become the symbol not so much of Love but rather of Law, self-righteousness and judgment.

But that is not the way it begins in Genesis. This special relationship appears to have two steps. The first is in chapter 15, in which Jehovah commits Himself to death should He ever break Covenant. It is remarkable that throughout the many and outrageous abuses of Israel within their Old

Testament history, even when He must discipline them, especially when He must "sit them out" in captivity, He faithfully honors this vow by steadfastly holding on to them. Yet in the end He will deliberately break this Covenant and therefore will indeed die (on the Cross) – but only because He is replacing it with an even greater Covenant.

Normally both Covenant partners will pledge themselves at the same time, but not so here. Although the Creator indeed pledges Himself, Abraham (Abram) does nothing but observe. For thirteen years he lives in grace, and only in chapter 17 does he now do his part by being Circumcised. This is the indelible mark to remind him and his descendents that the bond is based on Steadfast Love: all who are so marked are connected with the God of the Universe; and yes, although they may wander from Him, if they ever want to return, they will not be refused.

Yet the puzzle is that although Covenant is the joining of Bloods, the Creator has none. None, that is, until a Bethlehem manger, where now He answers this dilemma: He becomes a Man and sheds His own Blood in His own Circumcision, thereby joining Himself to all who are and have been in Covenant. Just like His death will touch all mankind throughout all history, so also His Blood can reach back to the very origins of humanity.

The Corrupted Image and Its Restoration

Love must be freely given, and therefore it must have the option to *not* Love. Although God knew what this would cost Him, yet He did not stumble at allowing this choice, since, for Him, only genuine Love in return would do. Of course, Adam and Eve take this alternative and rebel against God. "The Image of God" has now become distorted and displays only the selfish chaos, not of its Creator's heart, but of its own [Mark 7:21-23], which then sets the *cosmos* adrift from its anchor in its Creator.

Surprisingly Jehovah does not reject His original design, but instead begins the process to restore His special creatures to their proper function in Creation. There will be discipline and the facing of the reality of their situation. God replaces their flimsy attempt to cover their rebellion, giving them a more lasting solution, which also points to the future permanent covering of righteousness in Jesus: the *Innocent Victim* of God's choosing will shed Its [His] Blood in order to cover not just Adam and Eve's rebellion, but eventually all humanity's sin. However, Jesus' Blood is so great that it is not "used up" in redeeming sin, but rather it makes alive and sustains all who turn back to Covenant with their Creator – in which now the Blood/Life/Soul begins again to *flow* between them.

No Trivial Connection

God wants this connection – even the eight-day-old child (the helpless) and the slave (the hopeless) are to be included. He is deadly serious about it – even His chosen deliverer of Israel, Moses, could not evade Jehovah's determination to have Covenant with each of His People, especially when that bond would provide comfort, protection and participation in the "salvation" events to come. It is not based on their ability, but rather on the compelling of His heart.

This is the foundation for the relationship – the better one – that He has in the New Testament. It is better not because more is required of *humans*, but because the Creator personally sets foot on this earth and gives Himself to an even greater degree – He throws Himself into this relationship more totally than we could ever imagine. Yet His heart has not changed – even with the eight-day-old child, "male *and* female" [Galatians 3:27-28], He still wants the environment of Covenant so that He may bless and show "the riches of His grace in Christ Jesus" [Ephesians 2:7].

6

2. *The Birth of God's New People* (See pages 57-72)

From the Side

St John records that at the crucifixion, when a soldier checks whether Jesus has indeed died, he thrusts a spear through our Lord's side into His heart and out comes "Blood and Water" [John 19:34-35]. At first glance it may be assumed that John's point in recording this incident is simply to confirm His death, which would then declare that Easter morning is truly a Resurrection.

However, his first letter, John speaks of "the Spirit, the Water, and the Blood" as *witnesses* [I John 5:8]. With the addition of "the Spirit," is there more to the "Blood and Water" than merely to confirm Jesus' death?

Reading earlier in John's Gospel, we come across two discussions. One deals with "the Water," the Nicodemus dialogue in chapter 3; the other is the "Flesh and Blood" teaching in chapter 6. Coupled to these is "the testimony" of the Holy Spirit, "Who witnesses of Me" [15:26], and we see that chapter 19 echoes with "that the Scripture might be fulfilled" [19:24, 28, 36, and significantly v 37 "Him Whom they pierced"] – this testimony is rooted not in what merely *seems* appealing, but in the concrete substance of the God-breathed/spirited Word of God. In Covenant terminology, these "witnesses" are the "signs" which declare that the relationship with God is established and available.

We have arrived in the midst of "the Word and the Sacraments" of the New Covenant – that new relationship initiated at that Cross – and the call is very personal to us as individuals: "*you* must be born again … of Water and the Spirit" [3:7, 5]

Born Again

We do not look, feel or appear any different after Baptism, yet something has indeed changed spiritually. In a very real sense we are a new species in the universe: St Peter describes it as "not of perishable seed, but of imperishable" [I Peter 1:23], "participants in the divine nature" [II 1:4]. It is this to which the Old Testament Covenant could only allude in its concept of one Blood flowing between the Covenant-partners.

No, we don't become God, but rather, as in the "participation" of Holy Communion, the Divinity that is Jesus enters into and unites Himself with us, just like when copper and zinc almost irreversibly become the alloy brass. Not only does Jesus "participate" with our humanity, but we also "participate" in the saving work that He does: crucified with Him, died with Him, live with Him, buried with Him, raised with Him [Romans 6:3-4; Colossians 2:12]. This also means we will sit with Him at the Father's right hand [Ephesians 2:5-6] – an eternity of this incredible privilege!

But this participation is far broader, since through Baptism, in Jesus all who are in this Covenant have a timeless and locationless unity and bond with each other which is unmatched by anything found in this world.

Children of God

It had been no afterthought, no "on-the-go" modification of the plan, but we have been chosen "in Him before the foundation of the world" [Ephesians 1:4], chosen to be adopted by the Creator Himself and nothing less, chosen because of His Love and Glory. It is "while we were still sinners … when we were enemies we were reconciled to God through the death of His Son" [Romans 5:8,10]. It is, as all matters of doctrine must be, Jehovah's idea first and we are to do it because He insists on it.

It is all or nothing, no foster children, no probations. Using the word "adoption" [for example, Galatians 4:5] is most significant for John and Paul's readers: in their culture, the adopting parent could never back out, never disinherit, never forsake this child – in fact, the Father could never do to His adopted children what He had to do to His "natural" Son on the Cross (when Jesus cries out Psalm 22: "My God, My God, why have You forsaken Me?" [Mathew 27:45]). To them, using the term "adoption" is a powerful statement that the Lord will always "be there" for His children.

A rich young ruler wants to know what he can do to inherit eternal life. The answer is "Nothing!" That's because at the Cross all has been done; however, only a child can inherit – or rather, an adopted child cannot *but* share in his Father's inheritance. Still it is not as if such an inheritance is reluctantly doled out,

> … in Love He destined us for adoption through Jesus Christ to Himself, according to the delight of His will, to the praise of the Glory of His grace which He freely bestowed on us in the Beloved – in Him we have redemption through His Blood, the forgiveness of trespasses, according to the riches of His grace which He *lavished* upon us …
>
> Ephesians 1:4-8

To be a "child of God" can mean many different things to different people, but to call the Creator of the Universe "Dad! [*Abba!*]" [Romans 8:15-17] with that degree of informality certainly must astound us. Yet that is the term that Paul uses. Now obviously the term can be used respectfully or with insolence, but used respectfully, we can "with confidence draw near to the Throne of Grace" [Hebrews 4:16]. And because we are "wrapped up in Jesus" or as Paul is fond of saying it, "in Christ," the Father's response is "My Child, My Beloved in Whom I am well-pleased!" [Matthew 3:17; 17:5] – because He sees only Jesus.

A family is more than just Parent and child – there are brothers and sisters! Yes, unfortunately (as one district president remarked), one reason we are called a family because we can and do fight like brothers and sisters. Yet there is a network of family that reaches around the world and throughout all the ages. One often does not have to go far to encounter a fellow member of God's household – there is help that surrounds us. It may be a physical help or a spiritual one, it may be an insight a brother or sister shares with us or something a saint from long ago wrote down and we "discover" it now. We also have the power and freedom to take our spiritual siblings before the throne that they may be helped and blessed in their need.

Taking the Name

Traditionally the newborn or the adopted are given the parent's "family name," which in this case is "Jehovah" – God's Covenant Name. The family Name is often respected or despised by the way the children live. Not only are we "the children of God," we are also His "Image" and "[Soul-] likeness." Have we taken this Name "in vain" or is it honored *because* of us? The gift of the New Birth is indeed a precious treasure, a wonderful privilege, and something that should also guide our lives.

3. The New Creation, the Bride *(See pages 73-86)*

The New Person

When St Paul compares the relationship between a husband and wife as reflecting the relationship between Jesus and His Church [Ephesians 5:30-31], he indicates that what we often think of as "the story" of Adam and Eve is actually a prophecy about our Lord and *His* Bride. Eve comes from Adam's side as a new creation who is exactly what he needs, so also the Church is a new creation which comes from Jesus' side, and perhaps surprisingly is exactly what *He* needs.

The Bride of Christ – as with Eve, she also is like nothing else: the children of God, co-heirs with Christ and "participating" in divinity; the Holy Spirit indwells her; she is Jesus' unique extension, His *Body* in this world. She has a different thinking, a different understanding, a different perspective – "the new nature which is being renewed in knowledge according to 'the Image' of its Creator" [Colossians 3:10]; "His handiwork … for good works, which God prepared previously that we should walk in them" [Ephesians 2:10].

With Baptism's "new Creation", immediately we expect a significant difference between the "Old Me" and the "New Me," yet it often takes time before "the fruit of the Spirit" [Galatians 5:22-23] grows in attitude, manner, speech, and actions. Still, the Holy Spirit's presence reminds us even in our prayers that He is at work and therefore the change in us is occurring.

So we find that after Baptism there are two natures operating in us at the same time: the "Old Me" which will never love God nor willingly do His will; and the "New Me" – or rather "Christ in me" [Galatians 2:20]. It is puzzling why Baptism does not simply abolish the old nature, but the Lord

11

in His wisdom chooses to have us wrestle between these two natures. Perhaps it is to remind those both in and out of the Church that we are not "too holy" to touch the needs of all people. Still, we share Paul's frustration as we find that "what I want is not what I do; but what I hate, this I do" [Romans 7:15].

The Tools of Baptism

Especially after Baptism, because we are aware of the new and precious relationships we now have, we are the more aware of how the rebellion of sin damages these bonds. Despite our disillusionment and even disgust at ourselves, "God is greater than our hearts" [I John 3:19-20] and in great relief we cling to the forgiveness in which He casts away our sins [Isaiah 38:17] and remembers them no more [Jeremiah 31:34]. In fact, we can now have *His* memory:

> … forgetting the things which are behind me and stretching out to what is before me, I lean forward toward the finish-line, to the prize of the high calling of God in Christ Jesus.   Philippians 3:13-14

Sometimes we have the sense that what we were yesterday is what we will be today whether we like it or not. But the New Creation of Baptism declares that there is no "yesterday" to which we are obligated. We are *new*. We can daily "return to our Baptism" by repentance and therefore repeatedly start out in the holiness that God has given to the spiritually newly created – we are not trying to crawl out of the swamp of sin with the futile and depressing task of "improving" ourselves, but rather in the pristine "newness of life" [Romans 6:4], with the Holy Spirit's guidance, we can choose not to fall like we did yesterday.

Satan, of course, will resist this victorious attitude toward life and he will attempt to resurrect the past, seeking to make us disheartened and fearful as we are reminded of all our failures and rebellions in our life. He is no mere annoyance but one who actively hates and wishes to destroy us in any way he can; but the ability of Baptism to teach us to forget [put behind us] what God has forgiven and be able to "lean forward toward the finish-line, to the prize of the high calling of God in Christ Jesus" is our effective counter to Satan's attempts.

Ultimately, Baptism is not merely a one-time event. Like birth it is the beginning of a process of intimacy with our Lord and dependence on Him that will never end, not even in eternity. This is no temporary measure which we will eventually spiritually outgrow; instead we will always need the help of the Holy Spirit and the relationship to the Father we have in Jesus. However, in this world, Baptism calls us to repentance from the emptiness and destructiveness with which our selfish and rebellious human nature infects our life.

Repentance is not a morbid activity as we often assume, but rather it is a great joy – it means release from the burden of guilt we experience. Yes, there is sorrow over sin, but repentance means turning away from such personal- and relationship-destructive rebellion. Yet to have such a repentance means that we must have a secure base – that of God's promises and forgiveness which has been established in the historical reality of the Cross. Without these things, repentance can become a terror and a despair; but with them, there is the joy of finally being rid of what has oppressed us for so long. And it is the solid basis from which we will share in the Resurrection and in our life "together with Him," life now, and life forever.

Welcoming the Bride

From Jesus' side flows the Water and the Blood through which the Church is born, a new creation which according to St Paul is also His Bride

[Ephesians 5:25-32]. This picture adds a very different "feel" to Baptism, since the idea of newlyweds and wedding feasts represents celebration, joy, delight, excitement, enthusiasm, anticipation and so much more. How unusual it is to think of God as eagerly yearning for the intimacy of a couple looking forward to their wedding.

Paul's passage puts these diverse images within the context of Baptism as he describes how Jesus personally washes His Church with the Water and the Word in order to present her to Himself without even the suggestion ("shadow") of sin, but that she rather is "holy and without blemish."

4. *Grace and Faith* (See pages 87-98)

The Nature of Grace

The very first thing that happens in grace is that God gives a promise to mankind. Humans could never start the process because: 1) they would not know whether God would be merciful to such rebellious creatures; and 2) they could never have dreamed that the Creator would actually give *His Life* for such tiny insignificant beings within the vast universe.

To this promise of grace, humans respond in faith. Faith itself is a most common thing, which we use constantly throughout our day. It is there when we expect food at a restaurant, buy merchandise, count on the other driver to stay on his side of the road, and so much more. Our faith guides and adjusts our lives, as when a doctor's appointment is made and we conform our lives according to the "promise" which the receptionist gave us. It can affect our time, meals, dress, transportation, thoughts, and the like.

The problem comes not in regard to "faith" but in *the Object* of the faith – by nature we just cannot trust God. Faith in the Lord cannot come from our nature which is suspicious of Him. It has to come from outside of us by the working of the Holy Spirit, the same as He must give us the ability and the inclination to face our sins and repent. In a very real way, this reversal of our rebellious nature, with such humble dependence on Jehovah, is simply a miracle.

Some have felt that the New Covenant was necessary to "tighten up" the requirements on humans so as to include only those who would be serious about their commitment and not eventually fall away. But this is not grace! Grace must always allow its own rejection because it comes not based upon human response but rather on the self-giving Love of Jehovah. What makes this Covenant "new" is the even deeper commitment *of God*, to where He would personally come to give *Himself* to an extreme degree, and would actually *become* the Covenant in the flesh.

The Old Covenant, however, can still provide a window by which we see His commitment and desire for intimacy in action. We see the depth of Jehovah's grace as He describes for His People *what He will do* – not in response to their activity, but rather as God declares in powerful terms to those in great need the impressive salvation into which He will set them.

Infant Faith

"Infant faith" can occur in a believer of any age. On one hand, it is the beginning of being acquainted with the Lord, dipping into the Word and tasting the goodness that is there. But just as it is not a good thing if a baby does not grow, so also the "infant faith," although still maintaining child-like dependence on the Lord, must move on to the "adult" aspects of our relationship with Him, seeking the deeper things of God, handling the challenges, and living the fuller life so richly made available to us.

This is a responsibility of the parents, who cannot carelessly "leave it to the child to decide" – it deprives the child of the environment of grace, mercy, Steadfast Love, forgiveness and the rest, which he needs in order to discover the richness of the life he has with the Lord.

Faith sometimes is like a tiny seed, so small that one may wonder if it is there at all. Yet faith cannot exist without leaving its evidence, although one may have to look carefully for its signs. There will be changes in life, differences in priorities and attitudes which will be in contrast to what the world has. Still, no matter how small it may be, a seed grows if it is a living one, and as we nurture it, it may indeed surprise us as to the size our faith can actually become.

Although we may smile at someone's weak faith, like Peter's when he walked on water only to become afraid of the storm, we all know very personally how easily what had seemed so triumphant in us suddenly evaporates. But the problem is not so much the weak faith in us, it is the Old Nature demanding that we must be perfect – after all, if we are going to try to "be like God," we cannot afford to show imperfection, even as we trust in our Lord.

We have forgotten that since faith is His gift, He is directly involved in its preservation. The irony is that even in weak faith we are called upon to trust Jehovah anyway! What a relief to know that He is prepared to handle our weaknesses with His power, and can even make our frail faith that which "overcomes the world" [I John 5:4].

5. Faith in Infants *(See pages 99-108)*

When we see a cute "innocent" baby, we are shocked to be told that he is in desperate need of a Savior. But part of this reaction is actually selfishness on our part. If a "pure" baby is not acceptable, then we who are less "pure" are really in trouble; if only we could make the baby acceptable, we might soften the condemnation against us. Unfortunately, we do not have such "wiggle room" – our "righteous deeds" are like "filthy rags," and there is no way to get "extra credit" to make up for those times when we fail.

"The righteousness of God" is what is required, which comes only by faith in the Savior. But can an infant really believe? Even being "blameless," which is how some are identified in the Bible, does not remove them from the umbrella statement, "for *all* have sinned and fall short of the Glory of God" [Romans 3:23].

Sin is very serious. It is rebellion and selfishness which rules one's heart. Even in the very young it is visible. As parents we do not ignore this sin – we seek to bring the child to repentance and to apologize to the offended person. We want the child to know forgiveness, especially the Lord's forgiveness; we want him to understand good and evil. We know that even in the very youngest is laid the necessary foundation for the years to come in regard to various aspects of his relationship with his Creator, Redeemer, and Helper. The child is most vulnerable because he does not understand about spiritual matters; therefore he all the more desperately needs the equipment which only the Holy Spirit can provide, which God provides through Baptism.

Human Inventions vs Divine Gifts

"The age of accountability" is sometimes brought up, but the trouble with this is that it is a manmade standard and there is literally nothing in the Bible to back it up. It is a vague thing – who sets the age? How does one know for certain "when faith begins"? Only the Holy Spirit can look into the heart to discern what we may not be able to see.

So also "Child Dedication" has no Biblical authorization. Unlike Baptism of which there are frequent references regarding its connection to God's activity, "Dedication" has nothing. Even in the odd instance of a child being dedicated to God's service (for example, Samuel), and the children Jesus commands to let come to Him, what is overlooked is that all of them *already* are in a personal relationship to Jehovah through Circumcision.

Considering Circumcision, we must realize that it also comes into being within an environment of grace, where God commits Himself thirteen years before Abraham enters through this action. The descendants of Abraham have been trained over thousands of years in which even the infant is to be included into this personal relationship with Jehovah. The Lord's yearning heart has not changed despite the change from Old Covenant to New – what has changed is the intensity of *His* involvement as He Himself takes on human flesh and *becomes* Covenant, uniting divinity to humanity *within* His Person.

"For It Is God Who Works" [Philippians 2:13]

Jesus does not set children before us [Matthew 18::2-5; Luke 18:17] with the idea that we are to emulate their *perfection*, but rather their *absolute trust*. He calls us to *faith* not self-righteousness. The irony is while Jesus says to adults that we must have faith like a child's, "the age of accountability" says *to that child* that she must be more adult-like before God will accept her into a personal relationship. Just because the child may not be conscious of her faith does not mean she has none, neither does a lack of sophistication mean she has none.

Even here, as with adults, the required faith in the Lord comes only by the working of the Holy Spirit, as a grace which comes to child and adult alike. We forget that Baptism, even Circumcision, both are passive events – these are activities which are done from the outside and the faith does not *make* them happen but ultimately only *receives* the promised benefits. The joy is that even though we must admit that the newborn is in desperate need of a Savior just like any adult, the solution is simple and is as at-hand as "the Water and the Word."

The Church has its role in this Sacrament. This organization is not manmade, even though humans make it up. It is a community created by Jesus Himself, His gift to His People. He has invested it with more power than we can even imagine. It has the ability to bring the working of the Holy Spirit into a person's life, whether newborn or adult. Those who are outside its Covenant relationship simply cannot access this power.

6. *The Body of Christ* *(See pages 109-124)*

Returning to "the Image"

The Creator has made mankind in His "Image," to be His reflection and "soul-likeness" to the cosmos. This has been lost in the Fall into rebellion, yet now in Baptism, the Lord affirms that His plan has not changed. We have become "the Body of Christ" – not a metaphor, we really are the living extension of the living Jesus. St Paul's use of "Christ" makes us aware of how he considers this to truly be an actual fact. As Covenant declares that through the one Blood, the same *life*, the same *soul*, the same *person* flows throughout each partner so bound, it is exactly that way between Jesus and us – even in heaven we will sit with Him on the throne! When Paul says "in Christ," he means precisely that.

Actually then, this goes beyond the "Image" as was given to Adam. Peter calls this "participating in divinity," in the same framework as when we participate in Jesus' gift of Himself in Holy Communion. Now, so joined to Him, we are His heart, voice, hands, and even His presence (living in us) in this world. In fact, from the throne of heaven we are equipped to surpass what He did when He walked this earth – *and* indeed there are many things He will not do on this earth unless we are participants in His work.

We are Highly Valued

Eastern religions declare that human "sin" is being separated from "the great ocean of life" by becoming *an individual*. The aim of their rituals is to make one give up this wrong thinking and be resubmerged into this great ocean. Evolution, as well, wants us to believe that we have no value, that absolutely nothing pays attention to us nor cares about us. In fact, the end product of its "billions" of years will be simply a *nothingness*. Both philosophical systems want to tell us that we ultimately have nothing to contribute, nothing we do is worthwhile – *we* are nothing.

Standing in contrast to these attitudes is "the Body of Christ" with the importance and irreplaceable nature placed upon every part – every individual – with no "vestigial" (useless) items. In Jesus' plan, everybody is essential, there is vibrancy when the unique contributions of each combine into the living representation of Christ.

Diversity

Sometimes we look on diversity with suspicion because "they are not like us." Yet the strength of "the Body of Christ" is precisely that range of abilities and tasks as Jesus reveals Himself into our world and our society. Not only are *we* valued, but we are being taught to value each other for the special ways that all have been gifted by the Head of the Body, our Lord. Sometimes we are called upon to humbly appreciate what the Holy Spirit has given, as so often happens when a crisis happens and the different gifts are revealed in what they do contribute to the general welfare of the Body.

Part of that humility is a coming to terms with the realization that *we* are not directing the Body (thank God!), but rather Jesus is. Because Jesus is indisputably the Head, the Body is far more effective (sometimes in spite us) in expressing the range of how He is there for us all in our needs.

The Care for Every Member – Large and Small

As we look at our own bodies, we are reminded that even the smallest member is very important to us. We realize this when we stub our little toe. So also Jesus cares directly for each one of us, even the little infant, because, after all, we are members of *His* Body! Through each other, He brings to

24

bear His wisdom (as seen in Creation and in our salvation), His love (as seen on the Cross), and His power (as seen in His Resurrection).

The members of Christ's Body care about each other because we are all in the same boat: we are all sinners. There is no room for pride. It can be the same kind of support as Alcoholics Anonymous and Weight Watchers have only "recently" discovered: that there is strength in sharing a common problem – and our problem is sin. On top of that, there is even more strength because He Who sits on the throne of heaven is One Who understands temptation even though He Himself never sinned.

Again, we are amazed that Jehovah would so strongly depend on *our* hands when He wants to do something in this world. Having received care from others, we in turn are the representatives of Jesus to those same people – there is an obligation for the mutual upbuilding and strengthening of all members of the Christ.

The Power of the Church

The Church has a secret power: its faith can bring the Holy Spirit's activity upon another person. In Baptism, or in Holy Communion, the prayer of the Body of Christ can change a life and change a person. We sometimes forget that the Church is not of human design, but rather is a creation of Jesus, and therefore He has invested it with extraordinary ability to bring forgiveness and other blessings into people's lives.

However, only this group of believers, who are destined to be His helper forever has been empowered by the Lord. The individual who may be doing the action of the Sacrament may spiritually leave a lot to be desired, yet the promise and the authority is placed upon the sum total of believers at that place: it is Jesus in His Body Who is working. This is why a rogue in the Church still can be used by the Lord, but a non-Christian simply does not have the ability to be Christ's hands – after all, according to Ephesians 5:26, it ultimately is *Jesus* Who washes "His Bride" with the Water and the Word. Even in the Old Testament, Circumcision is seen as the passing on to the next generation what *God's People* possessed.

7. The Kingdom of God (See pages 125-142)

What Citizenship Means

What does it mean to be a citizen in a country? It is a necessary protection for a person who is vulnerable to forces much larger than himself. It also means, in some countries at least, a guarantee of his rights even when that country itself has infringed or abused those rights. There can be a wealth of privileges which are available even to the youngest member simply by being born into a country. Yet the country also has rights, for example, to call on its citizens to provide for what is needed to defend or maintain the nation.

Heavenly Citizenship

Our membership in God's Kingdom parallels what we have on earth. The King of the Universe can call out His "Armed Forces" – His holy angels – for our sake (although since He includes eternity in the picture, He may not act in quite the way we expect). How good it is to know that He Himself has experienced injustice, abuse, persecution and even death, so that whatever our situation may be, it will not be out of His control nor will He be insensitive to our distress.

The heavenly Kingdom also has its "Charter of Freedoms" in Romans 4 through 8 – freedom from hopelessness, God's wrath, guilt (judgment), sin, the Law (condemned), death, weakness – guaranteed to all citizens. The true extent of these freedoms, however, will only come once we set foot in the Kingdom itself.

And, of course, there are all sorts of privileges that come when God is the Head of the eternal country to which we belong, as He bends the powers of the universe in our favor. Yet the greatest privilege of all is that we have become the dwelling place of the Holy Spirit, with the security of knowing that God goes with us and is always part of our day, no matter where on earth we may find ourselves.

Like any other country, this one depends on its citizens to contribute toward the country's welfare. However, this is a bit different, because the King is in us, working through us – He is determined to make us necessary participants so that we will reflect Him and will also share in the joy of His accomplishments.

He gives to us so that we might then pass on the support and the ability so that others are empowered to do the tasks set before them. In everything we do, we represent the King – we are His ambassadors – so that others may get to discover Him and learn what He really is all about. We are called upon to be trained, to be prepared to defend and to declare the King we have come to know and love. We also want to promote the local arm of the Kingdom's community life, developing responsible leadership, practicing fellowship, and supporting each other in their joys and needs.

Sadly, citizenship can be lost through foolishness or neglect, but the King does not give up on us. It is important, then, to pass on to our children the value, the benefits, and the responsibilities so that they also learn to treasure this eternal citizenship.

The Kingdom of Priests

The Creator always had the plan that humans were to be the pivotal intermediary between Himself and Creation – we would be the priests for all this universe's creatures, calling even the mountains and trees to worship, taking their praise to the Lord, and carrying back to Creation His will and blessings. However, the rebellion of sin changed this picture – the connections were all broken.

Still Jehovah did not give up. When He set before Israel His plan that they be "a nation of priests," they were too occupied with their own selfish concerns, and so lost this privilege. However, a Man has come Who has taken the position as the perfect High Priest. The dream of "a nation of priests" still remains, but this will be His Body, His Church, His Kingdom who will step into that meeting place between God and His Creation.

The Old Testament priests, as keepers of the People's connection with the Lord, were responsible for the sacrifices, particularly the *Sin Offering* (for forgiveness), the *Whole Burnt Offering* (the dedication of oneself to Jehovah), the *Peace Offering* (a communion between God, the offerer, and the priest/community), and the *Thank Offerings.*

The *Sin Offering* has been accomplished once, for all, for all time, by Jesus on the Cross. St Paul then calls upon us, as New Testament *Royal Priests,* to be living sacrifices, dedicating our bodies and renewing our minds, and thus being transformed for His service [Romans 12:1-2]. It is equivalent to the *Whole Burnt Offering,* the commitment of oneself – one's body – to the service of our Lord, the acceptance of being the dwelling place of God the Holy Spirit. This is not an easy thing to do, because our Old Nature fights "tooth-and-nail" against the Lord having such control over us.

The other half of this sacrifice is the adjustment of the mind: learning to see through God's eyes, discovering what it means to lean on Him, and not following the desires of the world. We are confronted with the humbling acknowledgement that we are not capable of doing this on our own; this can only be done in the presence of the Holy Spirit as Jesus enfolds us into *His* sacrifice, thereby making our gift effective and God-pleasing.

The *Peace Offering's* name comes from *"Shalom"* which actually means "wholeness," which comes only through the self-giving of Jesus to us as demonstrated in Holy Communion. The *Thank Offering* is declared in the communion service's name *Eucharist* (Thanksgiving) which bids us to "always and everywhere thank You, holy Lord, almighty Father, everlasting God."

This priesthood is not just for ourselves, though. The design has always been that we touch others and all Creation with this renewed mind and subdued body. Yet as we consider the ordination of the priests of the Old Testament, it is revealed that the Blood of the Sacrifice (Jesus) enables us to listen, work, and live (walk) as God's priests on this earth. This is where the continuing enabling of Holy Communion is so necessary week-by-week, month-by-month, renewing and reaffirming our connection though this Blood.

And as the Blood of the Old Testament's ordination sacrifice was mixed with the anointing oil, so also does the Holy Spirit "anoint" us, working with us to empower us daily to indeed be the very priests that Jehovah has always known He would have.

The ordination sacrifice parallels the cleansing sacrifices of healed lepers, and we who have been touched with "the living death" of our sinful rebellion discover that here also we are healed. Where lepers were despised and abhorred, now through Jesus we are not just accepted, we are chosen to actually be the ones God wants to us to be – the link through Jesus to all the universe.

And it is in this context when others observing us will also say of us, "They have been with Jesus!" [Acts 4:13].

8. *Methods and Rituals* (See pages 141-154)

Methods

There can be many arguments about THE correct way to Baptize. What gets neglected is that Jehovah's ultimate concern is over the relationship and not so much on the mechanics. His heartfelt yearning is to be connected to us; the method is only and merely the vehicle. It is true that certain elements in this Sacrament are unavoidable: the Water, the Word, and the Spirit; also repentance and faith, which receives the promises.

This is not to say that methods cannot be useful in order to highlight blessings and promises, but they do nothing to increase or decrease this gift of grace. What is sad is that some arguments are based upon what is locally available, attempting to compel all situations to conform to a luxury that is at hand. So for example, some will fight perhaps to the death about full immersion as the only way to Baptize, but what about the desert nomad or the Eskimo? What about the bedridden or others who have health conditions where this could be very dangerous, unless some sort of sophisticated equipment is used? But did the early Christians really have such sophisticated equipment? And what about hostile settings, where being a Christian is life-threatening and must be done in secret?

The issue is how pivotal Baptism is. If it is left to some convenient time, we act as if this Sacrament is really incidental. But that is not the attitude in the Book of Acts, where applying the Water and the Word is to be done immediately if not sooner. Jesus is vehement: "unless one is born again, he cannot see the Kingdom of God" [John 3:3]. Ultimately we do this action simply and powerfully because *God wants it.*

There are different ways to apply the water. "Baptize" itself can mean to submerge, to bath, to wash. "Wash" is another word that is used as when Jesus washes His Bride, the Church, "with the Water and the Word" [Ephesians 5:25-26]. "Pouring out" is yet another description which matches the "pouring out" of the Spirit in Acts 2:17-18, 33 [Joel 2:28-29], and even "sprinkling" can have its day, according to Hebrews 10:22.

The main disagreement centers around submersion or "immersion." Nowhere does the Bible say that any Baptism was done in this way – the passages that are used are often platforms for assumptions, not proofs. There are many problems with such assumptions. Archaeologists tell us that when three thousand were Baptized on Pentecost, there was no place available with enough water to use such a method. Even early Christian artwork depicts people perhaps standing in water, but water is still *poured* over the head.

This is never to say that immersion should be thrown out. As understood in "recent" theology (the last five hundred years or so), it is a valuable description of one of the concepts in Baptism, that of dying and rising. However, this is not the only important concept that Baptism contains. The other methods also depict valuable insights in regard to what God does in this Sacrament. Perhaps, where conditions and circumstances permit, Baptisms in a congregation might rotate through the various methods as a teaching tool to the people.

Rituals

Sometimes we see someone make "the Sign of the Cross" over his heart. "Sign," of course, is often a Covenant word which indicates the indelible scar left after cutting the skin to mingle the Bloods. The "Sign" has two functions: on one hand it is a comfort to the Covenant participant, because it declares that there is someone else who stands with him, someone on whom he can rely no matter what the situation may be – reminiscent of the wedding vow, "For better and for worse, for richer and for poorer, in sickness and in health" – and that he will do the same for his Covenant partner. On the other hand, the Sign is also a warning for an enemy that there is one who will defend and even avenge any harm done to this Covenant partner. In the Old Testament, the Covenant impossible-to-remove Sign was Circumcision: "in your flesh for an everlasting Covenant" [Genesis 17:13].

In Baptism, even the infant is marked with an invisible yet indelible Sign: the Sign of the Cross "both upon the forehead and upon the heart." It is the proclamation to the universe, angel and devil alike, that this person is *Jehovah's!* It is God's comfort to the individual that she is indeed the Lord's, and *anything* that trifles with her will have to answer to the Almighty Himself. It is the reassurance that the extraordinary relationship which has been discussed throughout this book unmistakably exists.

This is no automatic ticket to heaven, but it is the consolation that if one has played the part of the Prodigal Son, the "royal mark" still exists, the welcome door is open, the Love of the Father is available.

Depicting the white robe of the righteousness of Jesus, some rituals will place "a pure white unspotted garment" upon the newly Baptized, indicating how God has taken us from the streets and made us properly "clothed" to participate in the grand feast of eternity.

Another custom is the give the newly Baptized a lighted candle symbolizing how she has received the Light of the World, Jesus, and that she is to be the lantern which shines Jesus into the world. But a special usefulness is that the candle is to be burned for each Baptismal Birthday, thereby creating curiosity in the child as to why he should have two

Birthdays a year. This becomes "the teachable moment" in which what is discussed about Baptism will "stick" with the child.

The other Sign that occurs in Baptism is the anointing of the Holy Spirit. This is the basic equipping for all Christians so that they may now embark on the new relationship fully confident of God's presence and help. The Holy Spirit is "proof positive" that we are indeed the Children of God. He is "the Earnest" of God, the commitment of Jehovah Himself to bring into reality all which He has started, all which He has promised – that God Himself is acting "in good faith" in regard to His intentions.

9. *Living Water* *(See pages 155-170)*

Old Testament Depth

The phrase "Living Water" does catch the eye. In the Hebrew, although "Living Water" could mean simply "flowing water," there is a different word for that concept. *This* expression gets a remarkable depth when Jehovah describes Himself as "the Fountain of Living Waters" [Jeremiah 2:13; 17:13] and in Zechariah [14:8] the end time would be characterized by "Living Waters shall go out from Jerusalem."

It seems that it is this sense which is deliberately used in the sacrifice of the Red Heifer, the specific method to deal with the powerful contamination of death – anybody even touching a corpse or those healed from the "living death" [leprosy] must be cleansed by this sacrifice. As Jesus was, the heifer was killed outside the camp, its Blood not poured out but burned with the body. The ashes would be mixed with "Living Water" and sprinkled on the third and on the seventh day, on those who needed to be cleansed. This antidote for death was as close to eternal as one could get: between Moses and the destruction of the Temple in 70 AD, only six heifers were needed. Jesus, with the "Living Water," is the seventh, final and everlasting antidote.

New Testament "Living Water"

John 7:38-39 tells us that the "Living Water" is the Holy Spirit, the same Spirit that together with "the Water and the Blood" from Jesus' side on the Cross [John 19:34-35] are "the witnesses" of I John 5:8, and it is this "Living Water" that will well up into eternal life. This gift of His Spirit is not a prize for conforming to some holier-than-everyone-else regime, but rather His presence is the natural result and gift that springs from Baptism – the promise which Jesus eagerly wants to give us as He equips His People to represent Him in this world.

There are times when the bestowal of the Holy Spirit is conspicuous, not as a normal act, but rather as a highlight to an important stage in the Church's growth. In fulfillment of Jesus' promise in Acts 1:8, "you shall receive power when the Holy Spirit has come upon you; and you shall be witnesses of Me both in Jerusalem, and in all Judea and Samaria, and to the end of the earth.," the Spirit makes a dramatic appearance – *witness* – whenever the Church enters each stage of outreach which Jesus defines: on Pentecost with the disciples, then when the Samaritans first enter the fold, when the door to the Gentiles is thrown wide open, as well when the disciples of John the Baptist enter into the New Covenant.

"The witnesses" stand in testimony of Jesus' work of salvation and the results this has for us, the awesome connection to God which is described in the present book. The Holy Spirit, bestowed once upon us yet a "forever" gift, is the ongoing basic equipment needed by all believers. Not some mechanical add-on, but a Living Person Who responds to the flow of our lives and Who empowers us to be the special People of God, the Body of Christ, the Children of God, "the Image" and "the [Soul-] Likeness" of God, which we are.

Indeed the bestowal is only once, yet we are encouraged to "fill up" on the Holy Spirit frequently through using the Bible and in mutual support and worship within God's community. So also Baptism needs be done only once, although there are many examples in the Old Testament of cutting subsequent Covenants (such as Jonathan and David's Covenants). In those cases, any following Covenants really do not change the relationship into which the first Covenant set the participants, but can provide reassurance, comfort and direction for them. It is similar to a couple having a remarriage ceremony on their 40th anniversary – their status has not changed in any way, yet it can have positive effects.

Likewise, if someone wishes to be (re)"Baptized" in the River Jordan while visiting the Holy Land as a meaningful sense of participating in the great events which occurred there, there is nothing Scriptural that forbids it. The danger, though, is that such things can foster a sense of piety one-up-manship over others, and therefore it might be well to discourage repeated Baptisms.

Actually, Jesus Himself gave us a better way by which to "participate" – Holy Communion! This is a "right-now" action and presence of our Lord through which He participates in our lives and we in His.

In Baptism, the floodgates are open – a flood that flows into eternity. In John 7:38-39, when Jesus spoke of the Holy Spirit as "rivers of Living Water," we find that "Living Water" is a major expression of heaven. What is pictured here is just another way God indicates His desire and delight in how He will come to "dwell with us" and "make Our home" with us [John 14:23]. Even in eternity, the Holy Spirit will "flow" through us in limitless measure.

So, Does Baptism Really Save Us?

This Sacrament is no automatic entry-pass – however, it does set "the whole of a man's life from birth to death" (and forever) into the promise and sign of the Cross. It is the dynamic encouragement to continue in this relationship and to discover the greater and greater wealth, the lavishness, which God offers to each of His Children, Christ's Body.

On the other hand, yes, Baptism "now saves you" [I Peter 3:21], but only because it is linked to repentance, faith, the "flood" of the Spirit and the work of Jesus. It is a Covenant connection that surpasses the Old Covenant, and is now the opportunity to directly experience Jehovah Himself.

In addition, Jesus' Baptism is a powerful statement: not only has He washed off our sin, the sin now clings to Him. And there is more, for we discover that in the mess of our sin, Jesus is right there in the water with us, as He fulfills "all righteousness" – *our righteousness*. Baptism is the reminder that Jesus not only saves us, but has made Himself part of our lives and our world.

Baptism's Ultimate Conclusion

God earnestly bids all to "Come!" The Church bids all to "Come!" A most wonderful relationship awaits – a whole future within the deep Love and extraordinary grace and mercy of God, a future that literally never runs out.

The Gospel of Mark ends abruptly and leaves the reader hanging, actually forcing him to make a decision and to write "his own conclusion" to Jesus' story. On that same note we also must end our discussion on Baptism. The only real ending to this book on Baptism is the one which you write.

II.

Baptism in Depth

1. Jehovah's Dream *(See pages 3-6)*

Reflections

The Invisible Creator Glimpsed

It does not take much to realize that in this universe, God is invisible. It does not have to be this way, because, after all, in heaven He is always "in plain sight." So why did He choose to be hidden, and if Creation is to catch a glimpse of Him, where is it to look?

On one hand, the Creator has left His footprints all over the universe by which one could follow His activity:

> For what can be known about God is plainly revealed to them – because God has revealed it to them! For from the creation of the world, the unseen things of God – especially His eternal power and divine nature – can be grasped and discerned by the things that are made...
>
> Romans 1:19-20

Indeed, there is ample evidence of His "eternal power and divine nature" – but where does one discover His heart? For that, the Lord designed a special *mirror.*

An Intimate, Personal and Purposeful Creation

> Then God said, "Let us make man in Our Image, after Our likeness ..."
>
> Genesis 1:26

The Creator Himself handcrafts a man from the dust of the ground, and places into his nostrils His own Breath [Genesis 2:7]. But the Hebrew word for "likeness," "*damah*," is of interest: it is derived from the word for "Blood" ("*dam*"). Then in Leviticus 17:11, 14; Deuteronomy 12:23, "Blood" is equated to the word translated both as "Life" and as "Soul." So this "likeness," or rather "'Blood'-likeness," has the overtones of "'Life'-likeness" and "'Soul'-likeness." In other words, this human is to be more than simply an agent of God in His rule of Creation, he would be the mirror where Creation could actually "glimpse" its Creator, someone who would not only bear His "Image" but would be the "likeness" of the very "Soul" and "Life" of God.

Even the man's – and humanity's – Hebrew name would be the reminder of this relationship: "*Adam*," (derived from "Blood"), who was created from the *adamah*, the "ground." So significant is this mirror, this "Image of God," that nothing will take his place; his responsibilities will be done by no one else – not the angels, not even God will jump in to take up any slack. Thus, if not done by the hands of a human, then clothing the naked, feeding the hungry, sheltering a stranger, touching the hurts of a person, taking ecological care of Creation, and so many other acts which reveal the heart of God, will never be done.

Covenant

Thus Begins the Bible's Backbone

Humanity is born of "Blood" and its key link to its Creator is by "'Blood'-likeness." This will be of essential importance within what might be called "the Backbone of the Bible," *Covenant*. Covenant is not "made" but rather is "cut" – as in the North American First Nations' "Blood-Brother" ritual, common in one form or another around the world, where the participants cut their hand or arm and then mix their Bloods by clasping together the cuts, thereby having a "single Blood" between them.

The root-idea of this rite of blood-friendship [Blood Covenant] seems to include the belief, that the blood is the life of a living being; not merely that the blood is essential to life, but that, in a peculiar sense, it is life; that it actually vivifies by its presence; and that by its passing from one organism to another it carries and imparts life. The inter-commingling of the blood of two organisms is, therefore, according to this view, equivalent to the inter-commingling of the lives, of the personalities, of the natures, thus brought together; so that there is, thereby and thenceforward, one life in the two bodies, a common life between the two friends: a thought which Aristotle recognizes in his citation of the ancient proverb: "One soul [in two bodies]," a proverb which has not lost its currency in any of the centuries.

H. Clay Trumbull[2]

The enormous implication of this is that Jehovah (His Covenant Name) would bind *Himself* to *humanity* in *this* way. It is not as if humans are *somewhat* on the same level as the Creator – rather it is bewildering that He would seek such closeness with, much less so intimately join Himself to, something so miniscule in the vastness of the cosmos. Imagine sharing your Blood with a cockroach, and having its fluids course through your veins – and yet even this does not capture the enormous inequality and humility in God's Covenant with humans.

Of course, the awkwardness here is that the Creator, not being a physical Being, originally had no actual Blood of His own. Therefore whenever Covenant is cut in the Old Testament, it must be done by proxy, for example by using "the Blood of bulls and goats" [Hebrews 10:4]. It would take a birth in a Bethlehem manger of One Who *in His Person* is both God and Man in order to have the required Blood – and again there is amazement that Jehovah would actually go to such trouble to make this happen.

In His own Circumcision [Luke 2:21], for the first time in the history of *the universe*, God actually, literally and fully now shares His Blood/Life/Soul in Covenant with humanity. Just as Jesus' death touches every human being backwards to Adam and Eve, so also His Blood shed in Covenant completes every such bond by God all the way back to the origins of mankind – just as St Paul indicates how the Israelites participated "now" in the future "food and drink" of Jesus:

> Moreover, brethren, I do not want you to be unaware that all our fathers were under the cloud, all passed through the sea, all were Baptized into Moses in the cloud and in the sea, all ate the same spiritual food, and all drank the same spiritual drink. For they drank of that spiritual Rock which followed them, and that Rock was Christ.   I Corinthians 10:1-4

If this future and past effect of God's activity is a puzzle, it just demonstrates how little we understand the fringe between time and eternity.

Covenant and the Glory

St Paul adds another important element to this discussion when he ties "the Image" – the "'Soul'-likeness" – to God's Glory:

> But we all, with unveiled face, beholding the Glory of the Lord as in a mirror, are being transformed into the same Image from Glory to Glory, exactly as from the Lord the Spirit.   II Corinthians 3:18

Exodus 33:18-19 provides an interesting definition of "the Glory of the Lord": when Jehovah is asked by Moses to show His Glory, His immediate response is *not* to emphasize His power, majesty or government, not even the honor and the praise due Him. No, He accents His goodness, Covenant relationship, grace, and mercy; and in 34:6-8, also His Steadfast Love, faithfulness, forgiveness and justice. These are the things which God indicates are the essential character of His Glory, and these are the attributes which the human "'Soul'-likeness" would then reveal to Creation.

Covenant's Soul is Love

"Steadfast Love" is an important key to understand Jehovah's dealings with humans – it causes Him from His heart to create humanity in a Blood

(Soul/Life) relationship which we would call "*the First Covenant*" and is the underlying motivation for all His other Covenants:

> God is not only able to perform what He pledged to do, He could be counted on to *also want* to do so. The Old Testament word, occurring more than two-hundred times which epitomizes His fidelity to keep His covenants is *hesed*, translated variously as mercy, loving-kindness, steadfast love. The divine attribute, described by this term, is liable to change as little as His omnipotence is in danger of running out of power. The believer is assured that "it endureth forever" and "is from everlasting to everlasting" [Ps 103:17; also the refrain in Ps 136:1-26].
>
> Walter R. Roehrs[3]

We see the reflection, "the Image" and "'Soul'-likeness," of this committed love when Jonathan and David cut Covenant:

> When [David] had finished speaking to Saul, *the Soul of Jonathan was knit to the Soul of David*, and Jonathan loved him as his own *Soul/Life*. ... Then Jonathan and David cut a Covenant,[4] because *he loved him as his own Soul/Life*
>
> I Samuel 18:1-3

The mingling of Blood/Life/Soul in Covenant simply declares the reality of the bond which Jonathan and David already have – a bond based upon a love as deep as their Soul. This is the essence of Jehovah's "Steadfast Love": there is no compelling of another to do His will, but rather it is His self-commitment to an extraordinary depth, in an incredible magnitude, and in a bewildering determination. Such earnest faithfulness on God's part is most vividly demonstrated in the face of human rejection and abuse, particularly in the Old Testament and as Jesus comes to earth:

> Because love must always give itself to and for the beloved. If love were to give anything else but love, it would not be real love. Now this little baby in Bethlehem is God. It is love, it is God giving Himself.
> ... When we realize that God is Love, Bethlehem *must* follow.... Because God is Love, Love had to give itself. It did give itself. The Child in Bethlehem was born because God loved the world.
>
> Berthold von Schenk[5]

45

This is also evident when Jehovah "cuts" Covenant with Abraham (for ease of recognition, his original name "Abram" will not be used) in Genesis 15:8-21. Part of the then-common ritual of this bond is that each participant passes through the remains of animals which have been cut in half. The idea is that the living whole animal represents Covenant, with its Blood coursing through the whole relationship. Breaking Covenant is like tearing the animal in half and its Blood/Life/Soul drains away, leaving merely a mutilated corpse. As one passes through the pieces, it is a statement that "this lifeless, shattered carcass is what *I am* if I break Covenant" – it is a pledge to die. What should have absolutely shocked anyone who heard about this Covenant in Genesis 15 is that not Abraham, but *the Source of Life Himself*, Jehovah *alone*, as "a smoking fire pot and a flaming torch," is the One Who commits Himself to *death* should He ever break this Covenant. This is Love which gives itself in total self-commitment.

Imagine a wedding where the Bridegroom says "I do," but the bride says nothing. The Bridegroom considers himself fully committed to the relationship, yet the bride makes no corresponding commitment and pledge for over *thirteen years*. This is the scenario in Genesis 15! Although Jehovah fully commits Himself to death, it is not until Genesis 17:9-14 when Abraham commits himself. In essence, God is saying, "Even though you are not yet ready, -I- want this relationship and I dedicate myself to it 'to the death,' no matter what you or your descendants do or do not do."

During these two chapters, this human enjoys the benefits of grace, until *finally*, now no longer merely a recipient, he enters into full partnership in Covenant by the Blood of Circumcision.

This deep Love within Covenants, as with David and Jonathan's Blood-Brother bond [I Samuel 18:1-3], reflects Jehovah's Covenantal Love – that despite mankind's abuse, sabotage, even apathy, despite having every most compelling reason to throw Covenant away, His Loving-Kindness – His Steadfast Love – persists throughout all generations ("endures forever" [Psalm 118:2-4; 136]).

> … the Soul of [Jehovah] was knit to the Soul of [mankind], and [Jehovah] loved him as His own Soul/Life … Then [Jehovah] and [mankind] cut a Covenant, *because He loved him as His own Soul/Life.*
>
> Paraphrase of I Samuel 18:1, 3

Creating this Covenant demonstrates where God's heart is. As the Bible progresses, the human has many problems within this bond. Yet the Creator never changes the environment nor the purpose of this ultimate of connections – He makes Himself always available to His Covenant-partner.

It must also be noted that the deep, powerful and extraordinary Love which is expressed between the Creator and His creature, when it is reflected in human Covenants, has nothing to do with sex. The only exception which includes that type of union is the special Covenant case of marriage.

Distortion

The Corrupted Image

Human existence is grounded in Steadfast Love, which through "the Image of God," is reflected outward to Creation as well as, in the circulating flow of Covenant, back to the Creator. However, the Lord knows that to give humans this responsibility also requires that they must have the choice to *not Love*. Even knowing that such a choice will cost *Him* dearly, the Creator nonetheless desires and pursues genuine Love from this creature.

Already by the third chapter of the Bible the Lord's Covenant dream is broken by mankind: Adam and Eve choose to question their Creator's motivations, doubting His goodness and faithfulness (His Glory), and rather than being *His* Image, they have their own ideas [Genesis 5:3]. Throughout the present book, with deliberate reason, "sin" will be referred to as "rebellion".

As we consider that first couple's fall, there is a pattern which we must also recognize in ourselves. It is necessary that Satan gets Eve to repeat the command in Genesis 3:1-3, because he is not interested in a mistake, an error of judgment, a lapse of memory, or ignorance. He wants the person to know exactly what is wrong and despite that knowledge to determinedly go ahead in full-blown rebellion. Consider when *we* have done something wrong – invariably Satan has made sure that the thought has entered our mind that "this is wrong!", where we even *say*, "I know I shouldn't, but ..." or "I know I should, but ..." Just like Eve, we, also determined that "the benefits" of our will are worth it, go ahead in full blown rebellion.

> ... the structure of sin in the human personality is far more complicated than the isolated acts and thoughts of deliberate disobedience ... In its biblical definition, sin cannot be limited to isolated instances or patterns of wrongdoing; it is something much more akin to the psychological term *complex*: an organic network of compulsive attitudes, beliefs, and behavior deeply rooted in alienation from God. Sin originated in the darkening of the human mind and heart as man turned from the truth about God to embrace a lie about him ... Sinful thoughts, words and deeds flow forth from this darkened heart automatically and compulsively, as water from a polluted fountain.   Richard Lovelace[6]

> For from within, out of the heart of men, go forth evil strategies, immorality/idolatry, thefts, murders, marital unfaithfulness, covetous desires, wickedness, deceit, licentiousness/shameless insolence, an envious eye, maliciousness, blasphemy/slander, pride, foolishness. All these evil things go forth from within and defile a man.   Mark 7:21-23

It is in this rebellion that Adam and Eve's "'Soul'-likeness" becomes distorted and, being now cut off from the Source of their "'Life'-likeness," they will die [Genesis 3:3]. Creation then, when it looks for the reflection of its Creator's heart, finds only chaos in the human heart and so it too becomes affected by rebellion [3:17-20], evil and corruption [Romans 8:19-21].

For those who thought they could blithely take over from God, the reality slaps them in the face; they realize how vulnerable and frail they now are up against Creation without their intimate connection with the Creator. Their effort to cover themselves with fig leaves (which rapidly deteriorate) is their feeble solution [Genesis 3:7].

Jehovah's Solution is Presented

However, God's dream is not thereby forfeited. That very day He comes to reestablish the broken connection between Him and the humans. He could have come sailing out of heaven, pouncing on their failure in order to destroy them. Yes, He does come with discipline, but more importantly He comes to restore, He comes with a promise and prophecy, He comes with hope. Yes, changes have come: they will suffer the results of their disconnection to life – pain and resistance will now be their companions [3:16-19]. And, because "the Tree of Life" is now a risk for them [3:22-23], they must leave the Garden or else face an eternity of this broken connection (which is what Hell is).

As so often happens in the Bible, a small obscure passage has great importance: "Jehovah God made for Adam and for his wife garments of skins, and clothed them" [3:21]. *This* covering has longevity, a vast improvement over the fig leaves. But these skins come from where? In order to have an enduring covering for human rebellion, an innocent victim of Jehovah's choosing has to die, to shed its Blood/Life/Soul, and then the Lord Himself clothes them from this sacrifice. Already God sets the pattern for *the Innocent Victim* (Jesus) Who will clothe those who accept His solution with *His* own righteousness [Revelation 6:11; Ephesians 5:25-27].

But also remember the Covenant principle that when this bond is broken (or "torn apart"), there is "lost" Blood, a debt of Life/Soul which must be recovered:

> A brother cannot at all redeem a man, nor give to God an atonement/ransom for him – for costly is the redemption of their Soul/Life which ceases forever – how can he live forever?...   Psalm 49:7-8

God's *Innocent Victim*'s Blood/Life/Soul will provide for a permanent ransom for all mankind [II Corinthians 5:2-5; Hebrews 10:12]. Yet even then, paying in full our "Blood"-debt is not enough – Jesus must also have abundant Blood/Life/Soul to *sustain* His Covenant-partners in life [John 10:10], a fountain which freely flows through His Word and Sacraments, and throughout the Life of His Church ("the living Body of Christ," as will be discussed later).

Circumcision

A Matter of the Heart

Aside from *the First Covenant* (the creation of mankind), Abraham's Circumcision is highly significant in the Old Testament. Unfortunately, by the time the New Testament is written, it has often become "the poster-child" for the burden of the Law and its judgment, but that is not the way it started. Almost *600 years[7] before Moses receives the Law* at Mount Sinai, in a powerful expression of His Glory and especially of His Steadfast Love, Jehovah binds Himself to a human on this earth, who simply lives under Grace for thirteen years.

When Abraham finally does his part, the action is not merely obediently cutting away a piece of skin, it reflects the cutting away of that which

50

prevents the "one Blood" from flowing between God and himself, that is, the rebellion of sin – yet note Who does this action:

> *Jehovah your God will circumcise your heart and the heart of your offspring*, [so that you will] love Jehovah your God with all your heart and with all your Soul, that you may live.
> Deuteronomy 30:6; cf. 10:16; 30:6; Leviticus 26:41; Jeremiah 4:4

> In Whom also you were circumcised with a Circumcision made without hands, by putting off the body of flesh, in the Circumcision of Christ, and you were buried with Him in Baptism… Colossians 2:11-12

This cut is not something to just "scab over" and heal, to become a mere memory, as when the body closes a wound and leaves a scar. As with birth and marriage, it is rather the threshold of a flowing relationship throughout each day, in every moment, into eternity – to be with every beat of his heart and Jehovah's heart in a literal oneness of Blood/Life/Soul.

Circumcision is Laced with Grace

Just as it is *the Creator's* earnest desire for mankind to be His partner ("the Image of God") in revealing Himself and His Glory to Creation, so also the intimate and personal bond of Blood/Life/Soul in Covenant is not by human permission, but by Jehovah's heartfelt command. This *deepest yearning of God toward humans* (after all, He would *die* in order to make such a connection an eternal reality) even demands the *eight-day-old* child and the *slave* to be equally included:

> The son of eight days old among you shall be Circumcised, every male in your generation, he who is born in the house or bought with money from any foreigner who is not of your seed. … My Covenant shall be in your flesh for an everlasting Covenant. An uncircumcised male who is not Circumcised in the flesh of his foreskin, his Soul/Life shall be cut off from his People; *My Covenant he has broken.* Genesis 17:12-14

Not based on human whim or supposed ability, the command deliberately includes those who are most helpless about themselves and it is a matter of Life and death: without this connection to Him, the person's Soul/Life is cut off from God. Why? Why is God this serious about even the helpless and hopeless person (infant or slave) being part of this Covenant? Why is the choice not vaguely left to the child until whatever time he might think it worthwhile?

The parent is given a grave responsibility – *HE* could bring down the judgment of broken Covenant upon his child! In fact, even the chosen deliverer Moses almost dies ("Jehovah ... sought to kill him") by ignoring this parental responsibility [Exodus 4:24-26]. We cannot imagine just how very serious God is about wanting this environment of Covenant "now." He does not want Moses' son or *any* of His People, throughout their lives and that of their descendants, to be merely "tag-along" associates to the great things He does among His People. Each person is to unmistakably *know* that it is *specifically for him* for whom God does His salvation event (for Moses, the Passover and the Exodus from Egypt). He is to *know* that the personally guaranteed comfort, protection and participation in what God does for His People *includes him* from the beginning.

Jehovah is not waiting until the child is "properly" motivated or adult-like – He specifically wants the environment in which *He* will pour out blessings special to this relationship *now*, in which environment faith is cultivated and nourished *now*, and in which one's spiritual life-skills are learned *now* in every step of life.

The Security of Covenant

What if some did not believe? Will their unbelief make worthless God's faithfulness? By no means! Let God be true and every man a liar, as it is written, "That You will be justified in Your words, and will overcome when You are judged." Romans 3:3-4

Paul's argument is significant: Jehovah will be faithful to His eternal earnest desire which motivated His creation of humanity. Grace *will not* be withdrawn. It *will not* be modified. That "some [of the Circumcised] did not believe" has never and could never compel the Lord to alter the very roots of His deep longing, which come not from human initiative, but from *His* heart. This is a comfort for those who have broken away from the relationship and question whether they could ever return (as "the Prodigal Son" is able to return [Luke 15:21]). The answer throughout Israel's horrendous abuses of Covenant in the Old Testament is that God holds fast to His side of Covenant: He never abandons His Covenant-partner. Even when they must have severe discipline in the Babylonian Captivity, they go with His firm guarantee that they will return.

Although God never backs away from His commitment, only those who remain in this bond will receive and experience "the breadth and length and height and depth, and to know the Love of Christ" [Ephesians 3:18-19], while those rejecting the relationship experience the sad conclusion of "no Life in you" [John 6:53]. But that second alternative is not His desire – consider the note of near desperation in God's yearning for the humans in rebellion:

> "As I live," says the Lord Jehovah, "have I pleasure in the death of the wicked? rather that the wicked turn from his way and live! Turn, turn from your evil ways – why should you die, O house of Israel?"
> Ezekiel 33:11

> O Jerusalem, Jerusalem, who kills the prophets and stones those who are sent to her! How often would I have gathered your children together as a hen gathers her chicks under the wings, and you would not! Matthew 23:37

A New Relationship

The Broken and the New Covenants

At first we would assume that "broken Covenant" always describes how we humans tear apart this bond, however in Zechariah 11:10-13, surprisingly – and shockingly – Jehovah announces that *He* will break Covenant despite His thousands of years of *faithfulness (His Glory)* in the midst of human rebellion. Having pledged Himself to death, it means He *must* die! However, looking at the elements in this prophecy, we realize that the context of this occasion will be Jesus' death on the Cross.

Why is He shattering the Old Covenant? He is replacing it with a new and better one, in which the Old and the New cannot coexist. After seeing Israel's faithlessness, will the New place more requirements on the human participants? No, there is no demand for better believers than Abraham, David, or Daniel; nor to walk closer to God than Enoch or Elijah; nor to be more committed than Moses or King Josiah.

Neither have the grace, mercy, Steadfast Love and forgiveness changed. That which drove God to create humans at the beginning, which caused Him to come on the very day of their rebellion to restore the broken relationship, which compelled Him to act in such profound grace to Abraham (and others) in the Old Testament, which obliged Him to hold fast to Covenant despite Israel's rebellions, is also that which demands that He Himself set foot on this earth in Flesh and Blood.

The Creator's commitment is what changes. Through Jesus' birth in Bethlehem, the New Covenant is marked by *an even greater involvement by God* – in fact, one might say that Covenant now walks around with two legs! *Jesus is the New Covenant*: literally *in Him*, two share the same Blood; in Him, God and Man actually become "one Soul." Cut Jesus, and Man bleeds – but so does God! Kill Jesus on the Cross, and Man dies – but so does God. To be "in Covenant with Jehovah" now means that one must be "in Jesus" or (St Paul's favorite phrase – over 80 times in his letters) "in Christ."

The Basis for Baptism

The Old Covenant simply shows that the New one is entirely consistent with Jehovah's heart right from the moment of creation.

This is why the motivation for Baptism is the same as for Circumcision. The Creator is still seeking a personal and intimate relationship with each of His human creatures – not for some future time, but for right now. His desire is to be intimately involved – even to where "He has both put His Seal upon us and given us His Spirit in our hearts as an Earnest/Guarantee" [II Corinthians 1:22]. Why do we see God as reticent, as if He has to be convinced to care about us? He knew what He was getting Himself into when He created humans. Nevertheless He is eager, delighted, enthusiastic about doing this, even when faced with His own death: "Who for the joy that was set before Him endured the Cross, despising the shame" [Hebrews 12:2]. That's why He desired even the eight-day-old child and the slave to enter under Covenant – so that they would stand, not outside with nose pressed to the window glass, but rather fully inside the environment of His goodness, mercy, grace, steadfast Love, faithfulness, forgiveness and justice – His Glory. *Every person is welcome*, whether "Jew or Greek, … slave or free, … male and female; for all of you are one in Christ Jesus" [Galatians 3:27-28]; *every person* is to see himself as standing inside, participating in God's great salvation events.

2. The Birth of God's New People *(See pages 7-10)*

From the Side

Blood and Water – Jesus has Indeed Died

In what seems to be another "small obscure passage," St John in his Gospel observes:

> One of the soldiers pierced His side with a spear, and immediately there came out Blood and Water. The one having seen [this] has witnessed, and his witness is true; and he knows that he speaks the truth, so that you may believe. John 19:34-35

At first John's comment can be easily passed over as merely verifying that Jesus has indeed died. Naturally, of course, this is important because it sets the stage for the Resurrection. Many right from the very beginning have wished to prove that Easter never happened:

> … some of the guard entered the city and reported to the chief priests everything which had happened. The chief priests gathered with the elders, and having taken counsel, they gave the soldiers much silver and said, "Declare that 'His disciples, having come after dark, stole Him while we were asleep.' If the governor should hear this, we will persuade him and you will keep out of trouble.[8]" Having taken the money, they did as they were taught. The story was spread among the Jews and is current to this day. Matthew 28:11-15

One claim is that Jesus is simply drugged and then is revived after He is taken from the Cross. This is foolishness in regard to a Man Who has been flogged especially by the Romans' ingenious whips [Matthew 27:26], Who was unable to carry His own Cross [Matthew 27:32], and Who has endured the trauma of crucifixion.

Also the Romans have probably hundreds of thousands of crucifixions under their collective belts by this time, and have literally seen every attempt to thwart this kind of death. Their solution, if they are in doubt about a person's death, is quite simple. A spear thrust into the side, through the heart will conclude the matter: either the condemned has now *become* dead, or the Blood will have separated into serum ("water") and clots ("Blood"), showing that death has already occurred, as is the case with Jesus.

This strong proof for Jesus' death allows "doubting" Thomas to have equally as strong proof for the Resurrection later in John's Gospel:

> Then He says to Thomas, "Bring your finger here, and see My hands; and bring your hand and thrust it into My side. Do not be unbelieving, but believing." 20:27

This is very important because the Resurrection is essential to Christianity:

> But if there is no resurrection of the dead, then neither has Christ been raised. ... but if Christ has not been raised, your faith is meaningless – you are still in your sins! I Corinthians 15:13, 17

In the sermons in Acts and in the letters of the New Testament, the Resurrection forms the key pivot of their arguments, and it is often the touchstone for offense [Acts 17:17-32; 23:6-11; 26:22-25]. After all, it is the guarantee that Jesus' sacrifice completely answered the need created by our rebellion, thereby opening the way to the Creator once again – the way to "the Tree of Life" [Genesis 3:24] – for all who humbly submit to the Lord's solution.

Blood and Water – the Three Witnesses

But John in his first letter also emphasizes that "the Water and the Blood" have more meaning than just to confirm Jesus' death:

This is He Who came through Water and Blood – Jesus Christ; not by the Water only, but by the Water and the Blood. And the Spirit is the One bearing witness, because the Spirit is truth. ... There are three bearing witness on earth: the Spirit, the Water, and the Blood; and these three agree as one.   I John 5:6-8

"The Spirit" with these elements are three *witnesses* – a "three-fold cord not quickly broken" [Ecclesiastes 4:12] – these are no mere *written* witnesses, these are the witnesses of God's activity within life – people's lives.

What is this activity? Reading earlier in John's Gospel there are two dialogues in which "the Water" and "the Blood" are highlighted, one in regard to Jesus' discussion with Nicodemus [chapter 3] about being "born of the Water":

Jesus answered, "Very truly I tell you, unless one is born of the Water and the Spirit, he cannot enter God's Kingdom. That which is born of the flesh is flesh, and that which is born of the Spirit is spirit."   vv 5-6

while the other is chapter 6's dialogue on "the Flesh and the Blood":

Whoever eats My Flesh and drinks My Blood has Life eternal, and I will raise him up at the Last Day. For My Flesh truly is Food, and My Blood truly is Drink. He who eats My Flesh and drinks My Blood abides in Me, and I in him.   vv 54-56

"The Spirit" of the trio is not isolated to a particular section of the Gospel, but as Jesus describes Him, "The wind blows where it wills – you hear its sound but you do not know from where it comes and to where it goes" [John 3:8], as He is sprinkled throughout the Gospel. He is the "rivers of Living Water" in the believer's heart [7:37-39]; the "the Spirit of Truth" Who "dwells with you and will be in you" [14:17]; "the Helper" Who "will teach you all things and bring to your remembrance all which I said to you" [14:26]; and He will be "the Helper ... Who witnesses of Me" [15:26].

However, the evidence that the Spirit bears is not based on upon inner sensations, as romantic as the thought may be, but rather founded upon concrete substance. In John's account surrounding Jesus' death, he is very emphatic "that the Scripture might be fulfilled" [19:24, 28, 36, and significantly v 37 "Him Whom they pierced"]. St Paul would agree, telling us that "the sword of the Spirit … is the Word of God" [Ephesians 6:17] and St Luke also associates the two: "the Holy Spirit fell upon all those who heard the Word" [Acts 10:44].

> After John records that out of Jesus' side came Blood and Water [John 19:34], in the next verse, he says, "The one having seen [this] has witnessed, and his witness is true; and he knows that he speaks the truth, *so that you may believe.*"
> "Witness(ed)" – although the Greek word is later adopted as "Martyr," it actually is not an unusual word … However, John uses this word group 45 times in his Gospel, 14 in his letters, 11 in Revelation – 70 times out of the 116 in the New Testament. It is an important word for him, and often it is in regard to vital spiritual foundations (for example, John 1:7-8, 34; 5:31-39; 15:26-27). So also, in both I John 5 and John 19, the "witnesses" of Blood, Water, and Spirit are defined as essential for faith in God's Son, … since they announce the intimate and personal flow of Life: "*This is the witness*: that God has given eternal Life to us, and this Life is in His Son" [I John 5:11]. …
> However, combine John's point that the "witnesses" form the grounding of faith, together with Deuteronomy 19:15: "by the mouth of two or three *witnesses* the matter shall be established"[9] along with "the Water and the Blood" as the "witnesses" that flow from the Covenant event of the Cross. In Baptism, then, "the Water and Spirit" take us to the death of Jesus and to the cutting of the 'New' Covenant, confirming this new Birth just as powerfully as when the physical 'witness' of Circumcision confirms the children of Abraham in the 'Old' Covenant relationship.   James Lindemann[10]

In Covenant terms, these "witnesses" are "signs." When earthly Covenant is cut, the result would be a scar, which would be the indelible badge of this relationship, as Jehovah declares in regard to Circumcision: "So shall My Covenant be in your flesh an everlasting Covenant" [Genesis

17:13]. This term is very important in the Old Testament, because a "sign" is the evidence of Covenant meant to be comforting to the participant, yet also warning to the antagonist: the "signs" given to Moses at the burning bush [Exodus 4:1-9], when done before Israel meant comfort [4:29-31], but when done before Pharaoh meant warning [7:10-24]. It is the same with the ten plagues later visited upon Egypt, which also were "signs" [translated as "wonders," "miracles" - 4:21; 7:3; 8:23; 10:1-2].

The New Testament "signs" or "witnesses" would be just as indelible, although not physically, but spiritually. They confirm one's relationship to his Lord, "witnessing" as "the Spirit Himself" does, bearing "witness with our spirit that we are Children of God" [Romans 8:16]. So the "witness" is two-fold, not just in regard to what Jesus has done, but also in regard to God's relationship and blessings of eternal Life to us, the "Life in His Son" [I John 5:11].

Therefore John does give each of this trio a very *personal* emphasis: "*you* must be born again … of Water and the Spirit" [3:7, 5], "*He* who eats … and drinks…," and "the Spirit of Truth … dwells with *you* and will be in *you*." John brings the believer right into the middle of what is called "the Word and the Sacraments." "The Water," "the Blood," and "the witness" of the Spirit do far more than merely testify to the fact of Jesus' death – they set us within the greater content of Jesus' work of redemption as they bring to each of us the promised blessings of the New Covenant.

On His Account

> Peter said to them, "Repent, and be Baptized every one of you in the Name of Jesus Christ into the forgiveness of your sins; and you will receive the gift of the Holy Spirit."   Acts 2:38

The *Theological Dictionary of the New Testament* [*TDNT*] indicates that "into the name of" has a certain understanding in the culture of the day:

> The formula *eiv to onoma* [into the name of] seems rather to have been a tech[nical] term in Hellenistic commerce ("to the account of"). In both cases the use of the phrase is understandable, since the account bears the name of the one who owns it, and in baptism the name of Christ is pronounced, invoked and confessed by the one who baptizes or the one baptized (Ac. 22:16) or both.   *TDNT*[11]

"This goes on His account" – what a rich thought this offers! As we come needing to be washed, for our sins to be died for, and so much more, these *witnesses* place it all on Jesus' account. He is the One Who pays the debt, and it is His reservoir which provides all we need for this life and the next. Imagine having access to that account! There is the wealth of God's Glory, His steadfast Love, His mercy, His faithfulness, His forgiveness at our and our children's fingertips. It also gives perspective as we consider these and other passages:

> In everything, whatever you do in word or work, do in the Name of the Lord Jesus, giving thanks to God the Father through Him.
> Colossians 3:17

> Is anyone among you sick? Let him call for the elders of the Church, and let them pray over him, having anointed him with oil in the Name of the Lord   James 5:14

Born Again

Of Water and the Spirit

"Unless one is born of the Water and the Spirit" [John 3:5] – Nicodemus didn't understand. Really, neither do we. After all, we do not look different, we do not feel different; to all appearances, nothing has happened. It is a good thing that Baptism does not depend on our grasp of what our Creator does.

Yes, there is a dramatic difference resulting from this action: under the creative power of the Holy Spirit we are born with a whole new spiritual nature – with a whole new set of *spiritual* "genes" from our new Father.

> Created originally in the image of God, redeemed humanity has been elevated by means of a *divinely conceived genetic process* known as the new birth to the highest rank of all created beings … Thus, through the new birth – and I speak reverently – we become the "next of kin" to the Trinity, a kind of "extension" of the Godhead … Here is a completely new, unique, and exclusive order of beings which may be called a "new species." *There is nothing like it in all the kingdoms of infinity* … But from all eternity God purposed to have a family circle of His *very own*, not only created but *also generated* by His own life, incorporating His own seed … or heredity … While we recognize the infinite distinction between the Eternal Son and the "many sons" born into the family, yet such is their heredity as the result of the new birth that He recognizes them as bona-fide blood-brothers.
> Paul E. Billheimer[12]

How staggering is the concept of the "new birth"! How utterly unique the Christian is – not just among humans, not just among the angels of heaven, but totally among the vast Creation of the whole universe! Not only has GOD made HIMSELF one of US, now *HE* has made US, *"not of perishable seed, but of imperishable*, through the living and enduring Word of God" [I Peter 1:23].

The Divine Nature

> through which He has given to us His precious and very great promises, that through these *you might be partakers (koinonia) of the Divine Nature*
> II Peter 1:4

Wow … "partakers in the Divine Nature." In a sense that should not surprise us, since the same message is in the Old Testament Covenants, where Adam is created from "Blood" to be "the Image" and "'Blood'-

likeness" of God, and Jehovah's Blood "mingles" with Abraham's – theoretically, divine Blood/Life/Soul "flows in his veins."

Yet it still makes us pause. It is OK to talk about Biblical people having that privilege, but it is a bit staggering to see *ourselves* "partaking in the Divine Nature." In fact, it is hard to *see* this as we look at our daily lives.

This can be confusing. It does not mean that we are God, nor that we become God. The Bible is pretty clear that God is a separate, thinking, acting Person Who as its Creator stands outside of the Creation [Genesis 1; Job 38; Acts 14:15; 17:24] of which we are a part. And it is just as definite that Satan's temptation in which we can become "like God" is built on a lie: "… Before Me no god was formed, nor shall there be any after Me" [Isaiah 43:10; also 44:6-8].

Although we are not and never shall be Divinity, the word for "partaker/participation" (*koinonos*, the root for *koinonia*) is particularly used within the Holy Communion setting:

> The Cup of Blessing which we bless, is it not a *participation (KJV: communion)* in the Blood of Christ? The Bread which we break, is it not a *participation (KJV: communion)* in the Body of Christ?
> I Corinthians 10:16

This participation is the pulsing, the heartbeat, of the Blood/Life/Soul of Jesus throughout His Body (which is the Church [Colossians 1:18, 24; Ephesians 5:23]). It is the "participation of the Holy Spirit" [II Corinthians 13:14, see Philippians 2:1], the "participation of the mystery, which from the beginning of the ages has been hidden in God" [Ephesians 3:9]. It joins all who are in this Covenant: "so that you also may have participation with us; as indeed our participation is with the Father and with His Son Jesus … we have participation with one another, and the Blood of Jesus Christ His Son cleanses us from all sin" [I John 1:3, 7].

It is to be fully immersed into the "New Covenant" – an *active* participation: "to know Him and the power of His resurrection and the participation of His sufferings…" [Philippians 3:10, also II Corinthians 1:7]. This true sharing of the Covenant-unified-participants echoes throughout the New Testament: "… our old man was *crucified with* Him … if we *died with* Christ, … we shall also *live with* Him … we were *buried with* Him through baptism into death, that just as Christ was raised …, *even so we also* …" [Romans 6:4, 6, 8]; "… *joint heirs with* Christ, if indeed we *suffer with* Him, that we may also be *glorified together*" [Romans 8:17].

The benefit of being united with "the Divine Nature" is that "I live – however it is no longer I who live, but *Christ lives in me*" [Galatians 2:20]. Not merely for the here-and-now, this most extraordinary level and privilege continues into eternity: "made us *alive with Christ* … and *'jointly raised up'* and *'jointly seated'* us in the heavenly places *in Christ Jesus*" [Ephesians 2:5-6], "If then you were *raised with* Christ, seek the things which are above, where Christ is, sitting at the right hand of God" [Colossians 3:1]. All of this comes to us in the instant we enter into the Baptismal relationship – because Jesus occupies all of this *and* all of us at this same moment.

> A good illustration of what we are trying to say here is that when two metals, copper and zinc, are combined under certain scientific processes they come out as a new metal known as brass. It takes more than just ordinary methods to separate the two, for they have become as one and that a brand new metal or alloy now exists. Now we are one in Christ Jesus united to Him in an indissoluble union. Consequently, whatever He is heir of, we have a share in. We are heirs of God and joint-heirs with Christ.   Theodore H. Epp[13]

The "New Birth" is not merely an illustration, but a reality. As Jesus is the unique combination of God the Son with humanity, so also in the New Birth we become a unique combination of Jesus and the Holy Spirit in us. Although never approaching the extraordinary oneness of God and Man within Jesus' Person, still as copper and zinc are melded by strong bonds, so He and the Holy Spirit seek to become truly one with us.

Children of God

"The Right to Become Children of God" [John 1:12]

> But when the fullness of the time came, God sent forth His Son, become 'of a woman,' become 'under the law,' in order that He could ransom those who were under the law, so that we might receive the adoption of sons. Because you are sons, God has sent forth the Spirit of His Son into our hearts, calling, "Abba, Father!" So no more are you a slave but a son, and if a son, also an heir of God through Christ.
>
> Galatians 4:4-7

"He destined us for adoption as sons to Himself through Jesus Christ" [Ephesians 1:5]. Within the subject of "God's Children" comes a powerful word picture, that of "adoption." This method of becoming a "child of the Father" contributes some profound additional elements related to Covenant.

The atmosphere of adoption is also the atmosphere of Love and with God, His Glory. Just as Jehovah chose Abraham for His Covenant, so also our adoption occurs because of *choice – not our choice, but His*: "He *chose* us *in Him* before the foundation of the world" [Ephesians 1:4]. This *"choice"* occurs as we are placed *"in Him"* by Baptism, and like Circumcision, this adoption is entered into because He insists: He commands it [Matthew 20:28]; He requires it [John 3:5]; it is His will [John 1:12-13]. He has no hesitation: there is no provision for certain achievements to first be made; there is no foster program, there are no probationary half-measures – His desire is "to go for broke."

And consider how in the culture of the Roman world, *by law* the adopted child could never be disowned, the inheritance could never be withdrawn – the adopting parent is "stuck" with the child, unless the child himself tears

66

himself away from the relationship. This is the *parents'* proof to their child and his security that he is irrefutably indeed theirs, just as in Circumcision, the child knows as he is growing up whose he is, just as in Baptism, the child knows *Whose* he is.

Birth of Privileged Ones

"One ran up and knelt before Him, and asked, 'Good Teacher, what shall I *do* that I may *inherit* eternal Life?'" [Mark 10:17] – what a most odd question: after all, one does not inherit by one's own deeds, but rather it is by the will and choice of the benefactor to his child, either by birth or by adoption. Instead, it is as Jesus announced, "Fear not, little flock, for it is your Father's *delight* in giving you the Kingdom" [Luke 12:32];

> He chose us in Him …, in Love He destined us for adoption through Jesus Christ to Himself, according to the delight of His will, to the praise of the Glory of His grace which He freely bestowed upon us in the Beloved – in Him we have redemption through His Blood, the forgiveness of trespasses, according to the riches of His grace which He *lavished* upon us …   Ephesians 1:4-8

> Faith has its place and it is essential, but only to grasp, hold, and receive the wonders that grace offers. The blessings of grace are for all, but only he who believes receives them. By grace then in Holy Baptism God opens His treasure-store and invites us to enjoy it by taking Him at His Word. So then God makes us His children, members of the Body of Christ, the Holy Church, royal priests, possessors of the divine nature, saints, righteous ones, members of the new creation.
> Robert Lindemann[14]

How extraordinary is the concept of "lavished"! It speaks of enthusiasm, of energy, of an unstoppable fountain of goodness – it is as if a dam burst and what had been pent up finally is released in a wondrous flood "of the riches of His grace" – released not because of better human cooperation, but because of *Jehovah*'s unique participation in the New Covenant.

Baptism is His solemn guarantee that He will never back out on us. If we need more assurance, one of the reasons why we have the Holy Spirit is that He is the Father's "down-payment" on His eternal commitment and promises. In other words, He will never stop lavishing the riches of His grace upon His children – *forever.*

My Father

> For you did not receive a spirit of slavery to again be afraid, but you have received the Spirit of sonship, in whom we cry, "Abba! Father!" – the Spirit Himself bears witness with our spirit that we are God's children, and if children, then heirs: indeed God's heirs and joint-heirs with Christ ...   Romans 8:15-17

"If children, then heirs – heirs of God and joint heirs with Christ" – what an astonishing thought: we are co-heirs, not with angels or any other created being, but with God the Son Himself.

> This is extraordinary! *"Abba"* – a child's version of *"ABBAS"* (Father), "Daddy" – is a term of familiarity and endearment. We run to the arms of the Almighty God of the whole wide Universe, He Who is above every angel and power and principality, He Whose Word creates and cannot be thwarted, He Who judges the world in righteousness and holiness – we call HIM, "Daddy"?? Yes!!   James Lindemann[15]

What boldness, what audacity, what comfort! We can "with confidence approach the Throne of Grace" [Hebrews 4:16]; with "confidence enter the Holy Place by the Blood of Jesus" [Hebrews 10:19]; "this is the confidence which we have in Him, that if we ask anything according to His will He hears us" [I John 5:14]. How is such a thing possible? Only because we have been placed into the "New Covenant," that is, into Jesus Himself.

We have the right of access "in Him" [Ephesians 3:12], and when the Father turns to us His response is "My Child, My Beloved in Whom I am well-pleased!" [Matthew 3:17; 17:5] because *we are "in Christ."* In Baptism "clothed" with Jesus [Galatians 3:27; Romans 13:14], God's opinion of and love for Jesus also then wraps itself around us as well [Ephesians 1:6].

On the other hand, Biblically, outside of Jesus there is no equal alternative – this awesome relationship with the Creator just is not there.

God's Child

> ...We can only understand and accept ourselves as servants of God after we discover and understand ourselves as sons of God...
>
> If you study Jesus' Parable of the Lost Son, you can see this point illustrated vividly. (Read Luke 15:11-32.) ... Had his father now received him as a slave, it would have been an act of love to save the young man from starvation. That was all the younger son hoped for; that was what he asked for.
>
> To his great surprise, he discovered that he had underestimated his father's love. When he went to his father as a servant, his father received him as a son, a lost son who was found.
>
> Incidentally, the boy's older brother also misunderstood his father's love.... He had things backward. He saw himself as a servant first, and because he served well, he deserved the rewards of a son.
>
> There are many people who think about their relation to God in the same way. They proudly accept their role as God's servants; they work hard at being Christian – obeying this rule and that law. Then they seem to feel that, having worked hard, God will reward them with good wages of protection from harm, peace without struggle, and a happy home in heaven. Francis E. Reinberger[16]

It is easy to forget that Baptism is not merely some sort of transaction, but rather a relationship of God's Glory as discussed in the last chapter. It means that rather than being stingy and reserved, God's participation is always ready, always willing, always able – simply because of Steadfast Love. Since "the Water and the Blood" both come from Jesus' side, then what Luther identifies in regard to Holy Communion also applies here:

> For just as one would act if ten thousand gulden were bequeathed him by a good friend: so, and with far more reason, we ought to conduct ourselves toward [the Sacrament], which is nothing else than an

exceeding rich and everlasting and good testament bequeathed by Christ Himself, and bequeathed in such wise that He would have had no other reason to die except that He wished to make such a testament; so fervently desirous was He to pour out His eternal treasures, as He says: "With desire I have desired to eat this Passover with you before I die."

Martin Luther[17]

Here is the Father Who reaches down in Love to touch the totally helpless and hopeless, whom Jesus calls "the poor in spirit" [Matthew 5:3]: those who because of their sin were unable to choose, unable to care for themselves, unable to prove themselves, unable to decide for themselves – but now "who were born, not of blood, nor of the will of the flesh, nor of the will of man, but of God" [John 1:13]. Just as physical children do not have the choice to be born, still Jehovah's intent is to set them within families so that they might be protected, fed, cared for, and brought to maturity. So also spiritually our Lord desires a permanent relationship where there is the freedom and security to grow and develop, even allowing for the prodigal child to go his way, yet where the Light is always kept burning for his return.

My Brothers and Sisters

> So then you are no longer strangers and aliens, but you are fellow citizens with the saints and members of the household of God
>
> Ephesians 2:19

The shared "participation in divinity" mentioned earlier has its role here: God's family means a network of brothers and sisters that stretches around the world, down through all the ages. There is help and comfort, encouragement and shared joy to be found, no matter in which corner of the globe we find ourselves. There is someone to turn to whenever things get rough or lonely. It also means that others will seek us out as they too experience the rockiness of human life. We can pray for and bring the help of the Lord to each other.

70

We do occasionally even fight like brothers and sisters, but the bond in Jesus Christ can make us pull together in time of need and distress, despite whatever differences there have been. We can come before "our Father" in prayer and bring His help to each other.

> So then, as we have opportunity, we should do good to all men, especially to those of the household of faith.   Galatians 6:10

Taking the Name

> Are not they (who mistreat fellow believers) the ones who blaspheme the noble Name which was invoked over you?   James 2:7

This is an interesting application of the Commandment against taking the Name of the Lord in vain. Through Baptism/Adoption we have "taken the Name," the family Name of our Father – it is no longer "James Robert Lindemann," it is "James Robert Lindemann Jehovah." Often a family name is honored or sullied by the way the children live – and since we are "the Image" and "the (Soul-) likeness" of God, this is indeed a significant aspect. Is our family Name "in vain" – useless, worthless – to us, and because of us, to those around us, or is it respected? Do we regard this Name as important enough to guide our decisions and manners? It is indeed an awesome, inspiring and dignified thing to bear His Name before the *cosmos*.

3. The New Creation, the Bride *(See pages 11-14)*

A New Person

From the Side – Adam's Prophecy

"The Water and the Blood" have one more connection, a prophecy which reaches all the way back to the second chapter of Genesis, where Adam's bride is created from his side [vv 21-22], and his response is:

> This singular creature[18] is bone from my bones and flesh from my flesh … Therefore a man leaves his father and his mother and cleaves to his wife, and they become one flesh.   vv 23-24

St Paul sets the stage for us to recognize this connection when he parallels verse 23, then quotes "the marriage verse" [v 24] and tells us that it is actually is a prophecy about Jesus and His Bride, the Church:

> For we are members of His body, "of His flesh and of His bones." "For this reason a man shall leave his father and mother and shall cleave to his wife, and the two shall become one flesh" – the mystery of this is great, and I speak concerning Christ and the Church.   Ephesians 5:30-31

In Genesis 2, Adam receives a new creation who is meant to be "exactly what he needs" for himself and his task of being "the Image" and "[Soul-] likeness" of God; now in the New Testament, through the Holy Spirit, from Jesus' side comes a new creature, His Bride, the Church. She is created by "the Water" and sustained by "the Blood," and will be "exactly what He needs" for the task facing Him!

Like Nothing Else

When Jehovah sets out to create the woman, as He brings all the animals to the man, He indicates that she who is coming as his helper will be like nothing else. So also, "the Bride of Christ" is like nothing else: these "Christians" are the children of God, co-heirs with Christ and "participating" in divinity; they have the indwelling of the Holy Spirit "Whom those who believed in Him were about to receive, for the Holy Spirit was not yet sent, because Jesus was not yet glorified" [John 7:39]; they are the unique extension of Jesus, His *Body* in this world – "the helper fitting for Him" [Genesis 2:18].

Although a different "new creation" than Eve, still "we are His workmanship, created in Christ Jesus ..." [Ephesians 2:10], with "a clean heart, ... [and] a new and right spirit within [us]" [Psalm 51:10], with "the New Man, which was created in true righteousness and holiness, reflecting [according to] God" [Ephesians 4:24]. This is more than simply reformatting what exists ("neither circumcision ... nor uncircumcision, but a new creation" [Galatians 6:15]); it is a different thinking, a different understanding, a different perspective; it requires "the New Nature which is being renewed in knowledge according to 'the Image' of its Creator" [Colossians 3:10]. In fact, it is a whole different life: "*His* handiwork ... for good works, which God prepared previously that we should walk in them" [Ephesians 2:10] – a new life in which "the former things shall not be remembered or come into mind" [Isaiah 65:17], "the old has passed away, behold, the new has come" [II Corinthians 5:17].

Same Ol' Me?

It sounds like the difference between "the before" and "the after" should be very dramatic and for some, the change in Life is indeed so pronounced that it can make us say, "Aha, there it is!" However, this kind of speedy makeover does not happen as much as we would like. For the most part, it is only over time when we begin to note differences in attitude, manner, speech, and actions that demonstrate that we have been infected by a new nature:

> But the fruit of the Spirit is Love, joy, peace, longsuffering, kindness, goodness, faithfulness, gentleness, self–control...   Galatians 5:22-23

Fortunately in the spiritual elements of our lives, such as in the ability to confess "Jesus is Lord" [I Corinthians 12:3] and in our prayer life, "it is the Spirit Himself bearing witness ... that we are children of God" [Romans 8:16] – we are reminded that He Who is the Earnest/Guarantee[19] [II Corinthians 1:22, 5:5; Ephesians 1:14] of God's Promises and salvation is indeed present and working.

But this seems strange. How can we be "a New Creation" if the "old" is still hanging around? If there is such radical "newness" (New Birth, New Creation), we should automatically expect to emerge perfect from our Baptism, but with dismay we discover that we are still saddled with the Old Nature (or "the Old Man"). I John 3 gets downright awkward: "All who are abiding in Him do not sin; all who are sinning have not seen Him nor known Him... all who have been begotten of God do not sin; for God's nature abides in him, and he cannot sin because he is born of God" [vv 6, 9]. Yet we know of nobody (other than Jesus) who can legitimately claim to be sinless at any point of their life – and if they do, simply ask their spouse or sibling ...

The Tension Between Old and New

First of all, it is necessary to discern just what John is talking about:

It is this new nature that is created in us in the image of Christ, a nature that "cannot sin" (1 John 3:9). It is the old man that sins, not the new. It is written, *"Now if I do that I would not, it is no more I that do it, but sin that dwelleth in me"* (Rom. 7:20). The believer is a person with two distinct, separate, warring natures: the old man and the new, the flesh and the spirit. Our sins, everything evil in us and everything evil done by us, are the works of the flesh. Our goodness, (if I may use such language), everything good in us and everything good done by us is the fruit of the Spirit (Gal. 5:17-23).

When God saves a sinner, he does not renovate, repair, and renew the old nature. He creates a new nature in his elect. Our old, Adamic, fallen, sinful nature is not changed. The flesh is subdued by the spirit; but it will never surrender to the spirit. The spirit wars against the flesh; but it will never conquer or improve the flesh. The flesh is sinful. The flesh is cursed. Thank God, the flesh must die! But it will never be improved. ...

I am not saying that the old nature is changed in regeneration; it is not. Flesh is always flesh. It never improves. It never becomes spirit. It only corrupts, rots and, thank God, in time dies.   Don Fortner[20]

It is not as if the Creator is not able to give us perfection when we are Baptized, yet how disappointed we are since He apparently chooses to have us still struggle against sin. This is not to give us a cop-out in which we can claim "my Old Nature made me do it" when we succumb to temptation. What is worse, is that since our sensitivities have been raised, we become even more aware of how the rebellion of sin has tainted its way throughout our lives and by just how much John's "sinlessness" is beyond our grasp.

We share St Paul's frustration in Romans 7:14-25, how we are a battleground between the rebellious, self-centered Old Me and the obedient, Glory-reflecting New Me (or better, between my Old Nature and "Christ in Me" [Galatians 2:20]). Realizing that in spite of whatever progress is made in "the fruit of the Spirit," as we wrestle with John's claim, Paul's cry escapes from our lips as well: "O wretched man am I! Who will deliver me from this body of death?" [Romans 7:24].

The Tools of Baptism

Forgiveness

But John does not leave us in despair. Truly, how easily and how often our hearts can condemn us, but "God is greater than our hearts" [I John 3:19-20] and "if we confess our sins, He is faithful and righteous, so that He will forgive us [those] sins and cleanse us from all unrighteousness" [I John 1:9]. He responds by casting "all [our] sins behind [His] back" [Isaiah 38:17] and "[our] sins [He] will not remember again" [Jeremiah 31:34], therefore "Beloved, since our hearts no longer have any basis to condemn us, we have confidence before God" [I John 3:21 paraphrased]. It is the same place where Paul ends up following his cry of frustration, as he begins His great Romans 8 chapter: "There is therefore now no condemnation to those who are *in Christ Jesus…*"

The New Birth and the New Creation, which come within the New Covenant, give us the reassurance that we can hold tightly to the promises of forgiveness, even in the face of our own self-condemnation; it is the ability to cling to the truth of "in this is Love, not that we loved God but that He loved us and sent His Son to be the atonement (ransom) for our sins" [I John 4:10]. And now as faith takes hold of such forgiveness, we become equipped to deal with ourselves and our lives differently – we also can have *Jehovah*'s memory:

> Brothers, I myself do not suppose I have laid hold of it, but one thing I do, forgetting the things which are behind me and stretching out to what is before me, I pursue toward the finish-line, to the prize of the high calling of God in Christ Jesus.   Philippians 3:13-14

New Start Daily

The assumption is that what we are today is the end-product of all the days before. There is a seeming obligation to continue to be what we were like yesterday – in fact, people around us can actually try to pressure us to remain the same sort of person that we have been. Often we picture ourselves as at the bottom of "the hill of holiness," where we attempt to struggle upward, fail and generally hopelessly slide back down. And it *is* easier to slip back into what has been comfortable for us, to the old habits which do not require new thought processes and new decisions.

But this is not Baptism. Nothing compels us to be "the same as we always were" – the New Birth and the New Creation tell us that we are a different person than we were even yesterday. There are no accumulations of habits, attitudes, dependencies, mannerisms, or anything else which we must uphold – we are not debtors "to the flesh, to live according to the flesh – for if you live according to the flesh you will die …" [Romans 8:12-13]. In reality, we start each day not at the bottom but at the top of "the hill of holiness," we are new, newborn, new creatures; we are what God has created us to be:

> buried therefore with Him by baptism into death, so that as Christ was raised from the dead by the Glory of the Father, even so we also might walk in newness of Life [that is, in Jesus].   Romans 6:4

No more weighed down by a past which now no longer exists, this is what Luther describes as "a daily return to our Baptism":

> It signifies that the old Adam in us, by daily contrition and repentance should be drowned and die, with all sins and evil lusts, and that a new man daily come forth and arise, who shall live in righteousness and purity before God forever.   Martin Luther[21]

What a different attitude! We have a different perspective on God and on ourselves. No longer are we desperately trying to strive upward from the bottom, trying to be "better," trying to fight past the overwhelming accumulations of the past; instead, finding ourselves at the top of "the Hill of Holiness," through the Holy Spirit we can now choose to not do the same things as yesterday, to not stumble like we did yesterday, but rather to have the New Nature take the upper hand. The focus is no longer on our failures and defeats, but rather now it is on those "good works which God prepared beforehand" [Ephesians 2:10], on what He is doing and on what He has made us become:

> Do not conform yourselves to this age but be transformed by the renewing of your mind, that you may confirm/reflect what is the will of God, what is good and acceptable and perfect.   Romans 12:2

> A dear pastor who heard of our ministry asked for an appointment. He said, "I have struggled for twenty-two years in ministry, and I finally think I know what the answer is. In my devotion time I read, 'For you died, and your life is now hidden with Christ in God' (Col. 3:3). That's it, isn't it?" I assured him it was. Then he asked, "How do I do that?" I suggested that he read the passage just a little bit slower. For twenty-two years he has been desperately trying to become somebody he already is, and so do many other believers. It is not what we do that determines who we are; it is who we are that determines what we do. We don't labor in the vineyard hoping that God may someday love us. God loves us and that is why we labor in the vineyard. We don't serve God with the hope that God may someday accept us. We are already accepted in the Beloved; that is why we serve Him.
> We must learn to accept what God says is true and live accordingly by faith.   Dr. Neil T. Anderson[22]

The Resurrection of Sins

We all experience flashbacks of things we have done or said: stupid things; mean things; good intentions that backfired; embarrassing moments; times when we have failed ourselves or at least what we imagine we should be like – and the list can go on. At times like this, our memories can be very acute; we writhe with embarrassment or re-agonize over the painful situations yet once again. We have repented – and at times, oh, boy, have we repented! – and have given them over to the Lord, Whom we *know* has forgiven them. Yet here they come again.

What is the source of these flashbacks? It cannot be Jehovah – He said "their sins and their lawless deeds I will remember no more" [Hebrews 8:12; 10:17]. But there is one who has a great stake in these kinds of memories: Satan. Dressed in a red union suit complete with horns and tail, he is regarded as a comic figure, perhaps a more or less annoying trickster.

But not so! The Devil is one who is filled with hatred. We catch an image of this in those people who will commit mass murder before committing suicide, or those who will destroy what someone else loves simply to watch the suffering. Satan knows the end that awaits him, and he is determined to bring down with himself as many as he can. He wants to kill, and if that is prevented, then he wants suffering and agony, the most exquisite of which is to make people so fearful that they are afraid to spiritually move. Reminded of failures and weaknesses, people become spiritually catatonic, unable to witness, unable to do much of anything for fear of "messing up again." If the Devil cannot win someone and cannot destroy her, then he will aim to make her so disillusioned and despairing so as to remove her from being any threat to himself and his plans.

Satan is the one who resurrects sins, often in our own consciences or through the revenge of the "offended." Our defense is Baptism with its powerful witness of forgiveness and of not just God's forgetting, but also of our forgetting, of what has been forgiven. Yes, the past can be humbling and there are lessons to be learned, but we do not have the time nor the right under God's forgiveness to relive and to re-agonize over what no longer exists in God's mind. The further confirmation is Holy Communion, where the Holy God from the throne of heaven, Jesus, has no hesitation to come and enter this sinful human creature, to dwell in us.

"It Ain't Over 'Till It's Over!"

> But we all, with unveiled face, beholding the Glory of the Lord as in a mirror, are being transformed into the same Image from Glory to Glory, exactly as from the Lord the Spirit.   II Corinthians 3:18

Baseball's Yogi Berra's comment, "It ain't over 'till it's over!" fits well here: although the one-time *act* of Baptism has been completed, Baptism is not finished. Like birth, it is only the beginning of a whole new life. It begins a dynamic relationship with Jehovah which should not end – *ever*. Even into eternity, the intimacy with our Lord and our dependence on Him will remain.

We seem to have an implicit assumption that once we are in heaven, without the defects brought by our sin, that we more or less should be able to handle things well enough on our own. Actually this is a variation of Adam and Eve's temptation in which they believed they could "go solo" and be just like God. The truth is that we will never stop needing the guidance and help of the Holy Spirit, we will never deplete our need for Jesus' relationship with the Father. At least, however, in eternity we will be paying attention and working without the resistance of sin which clouds our present relationship.

In the meantime, as we become closer to our Lord and become more conscious of how all is not right with us, Luther's "daily contrition and repentance" becomes a growing necessity. These are not merely mechanical things which a Christian must do, but actually what drives us to repentance is the mutual desire for intimacy between Jehovah and ourselves and the ways our Old Nature's rebellions have sabotaged this desire. Faced with the emptiness and destruction of our selfishnesses, we yearn to clean away what hinders and hides Jehovah's heart and earnest desire. Hence repentance can never be separated from Baptism's continuous journey into a fuller experience of the Lord's Covenant and Glory

> You have put off the Old Man, which (according to your former behavior) is corrupt through deceitful lusts, now *be renewed in the spirit of your mind* – you have put on the New Man, created in true righteousness and holiness which reflects God.
>
> Ephesians 4:22-24; see II Corinthians 5:17

Which Comes First: Repentance or Forgiveness?

Sometimes repentance is portrayed as a dismal, gloomy and fearful chore. Confessions are written which sound like we must plead with our Lord, as if He is reluctant and therefore our forgiveness is on shaky ground. This may reflect a concern that if we make repentance too easy, then one could become flippant about forgiveness. Truly, repentance is not merely mouthing the word "sorry!" and then merely walking away. Rather it is to increasingly detest how sin ruins the relationships which surround us, it is to reject how our rebellions lead us away from the Lord, it is to despise what we have become as compared to what we were created for. It is the earnest desire that things need to be different, that we want to come closer to our God and to our neighbors. We earnestly desire to see a change.

Yet at the same time, there is the realization that our forgiveness is not gauged upon the eloquence of our repentance, nor its apparent fervency, nor its precise enumeration of each sin – it is dictated by the heartfelt desire of the Father Who would send His Son to do what humanity could never do for itself. The forgiveness is an already accomplished fact. Jesus has needed to die only once for all time, for all humans, for all sin [Hebrews 9:24-28]. This forgiveness precedes our repentance, which changes the perspective on our act of contrition.

The Joy of Repentance

On one hand it is proper to sorrow over our sin. But repentance, for the Christian, is a joy! Repentance means freedom and release; it means a fresh start; it means a renewed intimacy with the Lord. That's because it has a solid confidence – it must have!

Without the security of God's promises and established forgiveness, we would be terrified of seeing the depth of our sin – we would be faced with the potential of utter despair with no answer. When Judas Iscariot realizes the extent of what he has done by betraying Jesus, when he turns to the only Old Testament place where forgiveness is supposed to be found – the temple –, the priests reply, "What is that to us? See to it yourself!" [Matthew 27:4]. Without Jesus as Savior (which apparently neither he nor the rest of the disciples yet comprehended), what could be more devastating than those priests' words? Having no other God-authorized place to turn, the enormity of what he did, and the inability to redeem oneself [Psalm 49:7-9] left him totally without hope – suicide was the conclusion to his utter despair.

When we are faced with the realization of how we also stand under the charge, "this Jesus Whom *you* crucified" [Acts 2:36], when we also are "cut to the heart" and plead "Brothers, what can we do?" [v 37], what a joy it is to have an answer!

> Peter said to them, "Repent, and be Baptized every one of you in the Name of Jesus Christ into the forgiveness of your sins; and you will receive the gift of the Holy Spirit." v 38

Forgiveness must be a secure option: "If You, Jehovah, should mark iniquities, O Lord, who shall stand? But there is forgiveness with You, that You may be feared" [Psalm 130:3-4]. St John reminds us that this forgiveness is an already accomplished fact for everyone in the world [I John 2:1-2]. The promise has indeed come first and now with joy we can get rid

83

of that which we detest, handing our rebellions over to the Redeemer, knowing exactly what He will do with them and us:

> O Lord, by these things men live; and in all these things is the life of my spirit – restore me and make me live! Behold, peace [*SHALOM*] was bitter to me, very bitter; yet You loved my soul from the pit of destruction, You have cast all my sins behind Your back.
>
> Isaiah 38:16-17

And so we have returned – returned to our Baptism, returned to the newness, returned into the extraordinary relationships in which He has placed us, returned to "participating in divinity." And we look forward to when we will live in this newness as a complete person forever:

> But our citizenship is already in heaven, from which we await a Savior, the Lord Jesus Christ, Who will change the body of our humiliation to be conformed to the body of His Glory, according to the working of His ability/power which subjects all things to Himself.
>
> Philippians 3:20-21; c.f., I Corinthians 15:42-53; II Corinthians 5:4

The Resurrection to Life

> In Whom also you were circumcised with a Circumcision not made by hands, in the casting off the body of the sins of the flesh, in the Circumcision of Christ, co-buried with Him in Baptism, in Whom you were also raised through faith in the working of God, Who raised Him from the dead – you, being dead in the offenses and the uncircumcision of your flesh, He has made alive together with Him, having forgiven us all our offenses.
>
> Colossians 2:11-13

Just as "the witness" of "the Water and Blood" confirmed the death of Jesus which paved the way for the proclamation and confidence of Easter, so also this fascinating passage unites Circumcision with Baptism and directs the outcome to the Resurrection. Ultimately repentance and forgiveness are the platform from which we not only participate in "the New Birth" and "the New Creation," but are also raised up into New Life "together with

Him" – the "abundant life" [John 10:10] both in this world and in the eternal future.

Welcoming the Bride

> Husbands, love your wives, just as Christ also loved the Church and gave up Himself for her, that He might sanctify her, having cleansed her by the washing of Water in the Word, that He might present her to Himself, the glorious Church, not having spot or wrinkle or any such thing, but that she should be holy and without blemish.
>
> Equally so, husbands must love their wives as they love their own bodies – he who loves his wife loves himself. For no one ever hates his own flesh, but nourishes and cherishes it, just as the Lord does the Church – because *we* are members of *His* Body, of *His* flesh and of *His* bones! "For this reason a man shall leave his father and mother and shall cleave to his wife, and the two shall become one flesh" – the mystery of this is great, *and I speak concerning Christ and the Church.*
>
> Ephesians 5:25-32

As St Paul infers, not just a new creation came from Adam's side, but *his bride* as well, so also not just a New Creation has come from our Lord's side, but also *His* Bride. This idea of "newlyweds" adds an especially refreshing aspect to what often are dry and solemn doctrines: a marriage feast in almost any culture declares eagerness, enthusiasm, anticipation, joy, delight and a sense of passion. Thinking about it, this is after all the Bride for whom Jehovah yearned from before the creation of the universe [Ephesians 1:4], the Bride for whom He has worked throughout the centuries [compare with Genesis 29:20,28], the Bride for whom He died, and the Bride for Whom He will return to take by the hand to the grand marriage feast in heaven.

Even in this perspective Baptism has its important role: "with the washing of Water with the Word," Jesus presents her to Himself, sanctified, cleansed, holy and without blemish. Unlike Cinderella who first is made beautiful before the prince falls in love with her, this Prince chooses His Bride while she is flawed and rebellious, and He is the One Who washes her (not even she herself can do this) with His tender, nail-pierced hands, and in the process transforms her into "a Glorious Church."

> He Himself scrubs away, and behold, what beauty emerges! The scarred, even downright ugly places in the Bride are not just cleansed, but actually are changed: the callused becomes soft; the decayed places rebuilt; the emptiness is filled – the Bride is created anew. All the painful spots He tenderly addresses, the stings and bruises that must be healed...
>
> What a vision of loveliness! He clothes His Bride with – Himself! "... that we might become God's righteousness in Him" [2 Corinthians 5:21]. She is truly a radiant Bride, shining with the Glory of God's own righteousness.   James Lindemann[23]

4. Grace and Faith (See pages 15-18)

The Nature of Grace

The First Move

> If a man is to deal with God and receive anything from him, it must happen thus: Not that man begins and lays the first stone, but that God alone – without any entreaty or desire of man – must first come and give him a promise. This word of God is the beginning, the foundation, the rock, upon which afterward all works, words and thoughts of man must build. This word man must gratefully accept. He must faithfully believe the divine promise and by no means doubt that it is and comes to pass just as God promises. This trust and faith is the beginning, middle, and end of all works and righteousness. On the contrary God must anticipate all [of man's] works and thoughts, and make a promise clearly expressed in words, which man then takes and keeps in a good firm faith.   Martin Luther[24]

As described earlier, "grace" along with other such attributes like Steadfast Love, forgiveness, and mercy are the elements to which God calls attention in regard to His Glory. These come not because humans have coerced them from Him, but rather they spring from the same motivation which caused God to create in the first place: His heart.

There is no way that a human could anticipate Jehovah's grace for two reasons: first, because he could not have imagined the Creator being that merciful. Like Adam and Eve, we tend to run and hide, expecting a "kill-joy," fearful of falling under judgment, leery of drawing attention to ourselves lest our secrets become exposed. Although we may want Him to be merciful, we have no ability to guarantee that He will be. No, He must reveal Himself as such by promise and by deed, and only now can we confidently lay ourselves upon His grace.

The second reason is because we are not able to think of the perfect solution. Who would ever have proposed that God should give *His Life* to redeem a rebel who fights against Him in every way possible? And the idea of the Author of all life dying at all is a ridiculous concept. Who would ever have thought that intimacy between the Creator of the vast universe and apparently totally insignificant humanity, so very tiny within that cosmos, would even be possible?

No, grace must always start with "that God alone – without any entreaty or desire of man – must first come and give him a promise," to which humans respond in faith.

The Miracle: Faith

Faith is a simple thing and we use it far more frequently in our daily life than we realize. When we have made an appointment with a doctor's receptionist, our whole life may be changed – that simple promise over the phone will affect what we eat, when we eat, what we shall wear, how we will get there, other plans that may need to be shifted, and so forth. In many other ways, our faith in *a promise* will affect our lives. Expecting food at a restaurant, buying merchandise from a vendor, using money, expecting the other driver to stay on his side of the road, and countless other examples minute-by-minute in our lives bear witness as to the constant daily use of faith, to which most often we give no thought.

When it comes to the spiritual realm, "faith" itself is really no different – what creates the problem is *the Object* of our faith:

> But the "natural" man does not receive the things of the Spirit of God, for they are foolishness to him and he not able to know them, because they are spiritually discerned. I Corinthians 2:14

Because the mind of the flesh is hostile toward God; it does not submit to God's law – indeed it cannot, and those in the flesh are not able to please God.   Roman 8:7-8

We are suspicious of God, and share in Adam and Eve's doubt in His motives and methods. This is something that has become very ingrained into our Old Nature, and presents a formidable barrier to trusting *in God*. Oh, we will still trust – we will run to the latest guru, to the appealing exotic religion, to the doctrines like reincarnation which we have shaped to please ourselves, to the psychic in the local carnival, to the horoscope in the newspaper, and even to the fortune-cookie fortune – to anything other than the God Who has described Himself and His relationship to us in the Bible. We will rely on the "scientific" philosophy which insists that there is no God to Whom we have to pay attention because there is no God to pay attention to us.

So if there is going to be faith in the true Jehovah, then it will not be coming from within us. Such spiritual faith could only be described as a miracle. It can only be something that comes from outside us and is placed into our hearts. It is a faith that can only come from the Holy Spirit.

> Therefore I make known to you that no one speaking in the Spirit of God says Jesus is accursed (or "Jesus be damned"), and no one can say "Jesus is Lord" if not in the Holy Spirit.   I Corinthians 12:3

> Not that of ourselves are we competent to judge anything concerning ourselves – our competency is of God, Who has made us competent to be ministers of a New Covenant, not of the letter but of the Spirit; for the letter kills, but the Spirit gives life.   II Corinthians 3:5-6

The Gift of Repentance

Equally so, "repentance" should also be considered a miracle, since to willingly face the depth to which our rebellion has burrowed into our nature and our lives, is repulsive to us.

On the other hand, repentance is a central motif in Luke's writings (e.g. 24:47; Acts 3:19; 5:31; 26:18-20). ... But there's more to Luke's emphasis on repentance. Take a look at Acts 5:31: "God exalted him at his right hand as Leader and Savior that HE MIGHT GIVE REPENTANCE TO ISRAEL and forgiveness of sins." And Acts 11:18: "When they heard this, they were silenced. And they praised God, saying, 'Then God HAS GIVEN even to the Gentiles THE REPENTANCE that leads to life."

For Luke, it is God who "GIVES" repentance. In Luke 3:3, baptism is FOR the forgiveness of sins. In Luke 3:6, John interprets his baptismal message as the dawning of the salvation OF GOD. This is an era that was not possible apart from God. As impossible as it may seem for infants to repent, Luke explains that repentance is equally impossible for adults as well. Repentance is simply a gift or miracle of God.

Andrew Das[25]

When Jesus declares that even an "obviously favored and blessed" rich man (according to the common notion) invariably loses the struggle against the not-natural humility which repentance requires, the shocked audience gasps, "Who then can be saved?" He replies, "The things which are impossible with men are possible with God" [Luke 18:25-27]. Old Testament or New, Jehovah must step into each life to make it possible for us to be saved.

"It is the Gift of God" [Ephesians 2:8]

If you would be saved, you must begin with the faith of the sacraments, without any works whatever. The works will follow faith, but do not think too lightly of faith, for it is the most excellent and difficult of all works. Through it alone you will be saved, even if you should be compelled to do without any other works. For faith is a work of God, not of man, as Paul teaches [Eph 2:8]. The other works he works through us and with our help, but this one alone he works in us and without our help.   Martin Luther[26]

What is difficult for us is that we want to have "our finger in pie" – we want to know that we are actively doing *something* in regard to our spiritual status. Actually, we want control over the Lord so that we can influence Him, compel Him, bedazzle Him. Like the nursery rhyme's Little Jack Horner, we want to proclaim to God, "What a good boy am I!" rather than to have the humility which exclaims "were it not for the Lord, we would have perished":

> But the tax collector, standing afar off, would not even lift up his eyes to heaven, but beat on his breast, saying, "God, be merciful to me the sinner!" Luke 18:13

We want our sins to be of no real consequence and our good deeds to command entry into our Lord's Kingdom. But as Jesus says to the church at Laodicea, "you say, 'I am rich and have grown wealthy; I have need of nothing' – and do not know that you are the wretched, desperately needing mercy, (spiritually) destitute, blind, and naked –" [Revelation 3:17]. We are so "spiritually destitute" ("poor in spirit" [Matthew 5:3]) that we could not on our own even say, "I have decided to follow Jesus," because our rebellion of sin erupts through our natures to that degree.

No, Paul reminds us, it is "not of yourselves, it is God's *gift*; not of works, so that no one can boast." [Ephesians 2:8-9]. We cannot even "throw ourselves upon the mercy of God" – we are as helpless as the person whose neck had been broken in a diving accident and now is a paraplegic who must depend entirely upon others – or as helpless as an eight-day-old infant, or as a slave. Jehovah must give us hope first and empower our faith before there can be any response on our part.

The Environment of Grace

Some think that since the Old Covenant "obviously failed" to make God's People truly obedient and godly, therefore a "tightened up" New Covenant is required, with more stringent demands and requirements, with the selection process narrowed down to only those who would most likely remain committed throughout their lives. In other words, the Creator "has discovered" that He just cannot be so free with His grace. But Paul indicates that such an idea misses the real point of God's grace:

> What if some did not believe? Will their unbelief make worthless God's faithfulness? By no means! Let God be true and every man a liar, as it is written, "That You will be justified in Your words, and will overcome when You are judged." Romans 3:3-4

The argument here is significant: Jehovah's promises are not dependent on human faithfulness – rather *He* will be faithful to His earnest desire no matter what humanity does or does not do. That "some were unfaithful" contrasts with how *Jehovah will not be discouraged* from seeking the closeness He desires. Rather than surprised and caught off guard by mankind's rebellion, *His* faithfulness to His Word is always the ever-present Rock, eternally unchanged and unmoved, always available to anyone who through the Holy Spirit responds to His call.

No, grace *will not* be withdrawn nor modified. God has not discovered that He must lay down a better law while demanding of humans a better cooperation; rather, the novelty of the "New" Covenant lies in the intensity of *God's* personal involvement – the nature of this bond, as in marriage, is how one commits *oneself*. He comes to personally, in human flesh, shed His own Blood, give His own Life, share His divinity like never before, among those who are helpless. Jehovah has come to actually be the Covenant itself, thereby fulfilling all its requirements, and now simply invites us all to enter and participate in His divinity.

It must also be remembered that as when humanity is first created, grace must always allow the ability to reject, all the while also empowering the responses of faith. Grace holds forth the promise that the faithful are to experience "the breadth and length and height and depth, and to know the love of Christ" [Ephesians 3:18-19], while those who reject this participation will receive only emptiness and eternal lifeless-ness.

I will ..., I will ..., I will ...

Besides, the Old Covenant cannot be so summarily dismissed: it reveals how the Covenant relationship stems from Jehovah's definition of His Glory (His mercy, grace and Steadfast Love), in a relationship that He has intensely desired, even when it would ultimately cost Him the Life of Jesus – and that intensity has never changed. Here in a window of His activity of the past, God shows what He will do within His commitment and within the intimacy of this relationship even right now.

It is fully in character, for example, to find in the promises of Exodus 6:6-8 a description of what God still does for His People of today, young and old, as indicated in the following excerpt from this writer's sermon, at the Baptism of baby Elise:

> So also, here in Baptism, Jehovah of the Covenant, Yahweh God, comes and says to a small individual, also in great need, in the words of the Exodus text:
>> "I AM JEHOVAH! I will bring Elise out from under the yoke ...; I will free Elise from being a slave ...; I will redeem Elise with an outstretched arm and with mighty acts of judgment; I will take Elise as My own People; and I will be Elise's God. Then she will know that I AM JEHOVAH her God, Who brought her out from under the yoke ... I will bring Elise to the land I swore with uplifted hand to give ...; I will give it to Elise as a possession. I AM JEHOVAH, the Lord."
> What a series of promises is made to her and to each one of us! ... In Baptism, Elise is taken out from being under the yoke of Satan; she no longer is to be a slave to natural desires; she has been redeemed with God's outstretched arm and mighty act of judgment to be found on the Cross and in the resurrection; He will bring her to His Land, the heavenly Jerusalem; here, God takes Elise as His very own person – she now becomes not just His creature, but His very own child; and He

becomes not merely some benevolent "fate" – "providence" –, but her eternal Father.   James Lindemann[27]

Indeed, "once you were no people but now you are God's People; once you had not received mercy but now you have received mercy" [I Peter 2:10]. In the resounding "I Will …"'s one can see God's powerful and constant commitment to His Covenant promises and willing response to any and all who turn to Him, despite even centuries of abuse.

Infant Faith

Baby Faith

A believer at any age can still have "infant faith." On one hand, this is good: "as newborn babies, desire the pure milk of the Word, that you may grow thereby, if indeed you have tasted that the Lord is gracious" [I Peter 2:2-3]; but on the other hand:

> I, brethren, could not speak to you as spiritually minded but rather as fleshly minded, as if to infants in Christ. I fed you milk, not solid food; you could not handle it then, but even now are you not able, for you are still fleshly minded. For where there are jealousy, strife, and divisions among you, are you not fleshly minded and behaving just like other men?   I Corinthians 3:1-3

> For when you ought to be teachers by this time, you still need someone to teach you the basics of God's revelation – you still need milk and not solid food! For everyone who partakes of only milk is naive in the Word of righteousness, for he is an infant.   Hebrews 5:12-13

We all start out as newborns spiritually, and it is important to have very basic sustenance in the early months. However, it is also necessary that growth must happen rather than spending our lives on infant formula. We are called on to move onward to the "adult" things of our faith, chewing on the deeper things of God, confronting the challenges of being Christian in an anti-God culture, and living a fuller life based on the results of the relationship into which Baptism has set us – yet at the same time maintaining the child-like dependence on, and delight in, the Lord.

> It may be questioned whether some theologians have a full understanding of the Means of Grace. So often they limit their conception of the means of grace to the receiving of forgiveness. Grace goes far beyond this beginning. Luther indeed includes all this and has the wider conception of grace when he speaks of "life and salvation." The abundant life is more than the forgiveness of sins. An adult Christian will not be contented with the mere assurance that he is not going to hell. He wants to swim in deeper water. Forgiveness is only the entrance to the ocean. The mature Christian wants to play around in the ocean of grace and exercise and have fun. The regenerate Christian is always in the state of grace. He has the blessed assurance and inner peace, "Jesus is mine." He can receive a wider and deeper appreciation of this life in the Blessed Sacrament. Berthold Von Schenk[28]

Parental Responsibility

This also why it is important for parents to carry out their responsibility to nurture and build up the faith of their children. It is not being bighearted to say that the child will be left on his own to determine whatever faith he chooses, rather, it is being lazy and irresponsible. That is like saying the child should be left to decide for himself as to who he wants for parents. That is foolish and very unsafe. How is the child to be nurtured and cared for in the meantime, and by whom?

When Jehovah of Covenant cares about this child and stands ready to lift him into His family, so that He may pour out the riches of His Glory (grace, mercy, Steadfast Love, forgiveness and the rest) upon him, it is absurd to refuse to have the child intimately know his God, to leave him unaware of Who it is that watches over him along with the wealth of promises which are available to him, as well as the blessings constantly showered upon him.

The Tiny Seed

> ... truly, I say to you, if you have faith as a mustard seed, you will say to this mountain, "Move from here to there," and it will move; and nothing will be impossible for you.   Matthew 17:20

Years ago, this writer's wife decided to plant a windowsill herb garden. She remarked how some seeds were so tiny that in order to move them to the soil, they had to be worked onto a fingernail and only that way could they be picked up. They were so tiny that one might ask the question, "Is it there or is it not?" However, what is important about a seed is not its size, but that it is indeed a *seed*. No matter how tiny, it can grow, it can multiply, and it can accomplish the reason why it exists.

The above passage comes to mind. A mustard seed really is not very large, yet Jesus says that if we have *that* much faith, look at what we could do. Conversely, most of us putter along with a lot less faith, and like one of the tiny seeds, we wonder if it is even there at all.

St James enters in, "... I will show you my faith by my works" [James 2:18]. Earlier it was discussed how just responding to the promise of a doctor's receptionist created all sorts of changes in our life. To discover what perhaps is a tiny seed of faith, likely it will not be revealed in grand feelings but by small changes in our life. We make the effort to go to church; perhaps there are some words we will not say; our conscience bothers us when we have hurt someone; we may choose to do different things than what we used to do or what those around us are encouraging. These may be "minor" things, but nonetheless they demonstrate that there is a seed there, a living seed.

Of course, seeds are meant to grow. We cannot be content if the seed itself never changes. Jesus also talks about the mustard seed from a different angle – the "surprise" of its growth:

96

It is like a mustard seed which, when it is sown on the earth, is smaller than all the seeds on earth; yet when it is sown, it grows up and becomes greater than all the garden plants, and produces large branches, so that the birds of the air may roost under its shade.   Mark 4:31-32

Weak Faith

But He said to them, "Why are you afraid, O 'little faiths'?" Then arising, He rebuked the winds and the sea, and there was a great calm.

       Matthew 8:26

Instantly Jesus, extending His hand, took hold of [Peter], and said to him, "'little faith,' why did you doubt?"

       Matthew 14:31; also 6:30; 16:8

What can be more embarrassing than to have Jesus look at someone, shake His head, and say, "O 'little faith'"? And this has been Peter's great moment of triumphant faith as he, Peter, actually walks on water in Matthew 14, only in the next moment to betray an appalling evaporation of that faith. We may cluck our condolences, but if the truth be told, we are too familiar with the same scenario in our own lives. We can seem spiritually noble and elated, powerful and self-assured, and then in what seems the very next moment we "crash and burn."

This in reality is our Old Nature raising its ugly head – not so much in the fading of our confidence as in the expectation to be perfect and in the conclusive evidence that we are not. Our rebellion against God insists that we *ought* to be like Him, perfect in every way, *even as we trust in Him,* and we despise ourselves for any and all defects, especially this one.

Ironically, it is when we have "little faith" that the answer is to trust God anyway, since in actuality He is the One at the control panel of faith – after all, it is His gift, His miracle:

Now if God allows faith to remain weak, one should not despair on that account, but rather recognize it as a trial and temptation [*anfechtung*] by means of which God tests, prods, and drives a person to cry out all the more and plead for such faith, saying with the father of the possessed boy in the gospel, "O Lord, help my unbelief" [Mark 9:24], and with the apostles, "O Lord, increase our faith" [Luke 17:5]. Thus does a person come to learn that everything depends on the grace of God: the sacrament, the forgiveness, and the faith. Giving up all other hope, despairing of himself, he comes to hope exclusively in the grace of God and clings to it without ceasing.   Martin Luther[29]

After all, if faith is a gift from Jehovah, impossible for us to create for ourselves, then He also must have a stake in its preservation:

Now to Him Who is able to keep you from stumbling and to present you before His Glory without blemish and with intense joy   Jude 1:24

who by God's power are guarded through faith for a salvation ready to be revealed in the end time.   I Peter 1:5

(1) The keeping for which Jesus prayed involved the eternal security of His followers. Our Lord had already spoken to His disciples concerning the frailty of their faith under fire (John 13:38; 16:31-32). Praise God that our future does not rest upon the strength of our faith, but in its object. Keeping is God's work, not ours. It is ours to abide (chapter 15), and His to keep.   Bob Deffinbaugh[30]

If we are determined to break the relationship, we can; but when we cling to the Lord and His promises, especially in regard to our faith, the task is His, for "What is impossible with men is possible with God" [Luke 18:27]. Humbly we discover that in His hands, even in our weakness, "… all who are born of God overcome the world/*cosmos*, and this is the victory which overcomes the world – our faith" [I John 5:4].

5. *Faith in Infants* *(See pages 19-22)*

The Desperate Need

Do Infants Need a Savior?

A most distressing fear is that even a cute baby could have sin. Is humanity *so* destitute before God that even a newborn baby would desperately need a Savior? And if he cannot stand before God based on his own innocence and lack of evil deeds, then we are even more definitely condemned, since we are far from the "purity" of the new-born.

However, if an infant could just "sneak" through, then perhaps some of our "righteous deeds" just might impress God after all – despite such passages as "all our righteous acts are like filthy rags" [Isaiah 64:6] and "the sinful nature cannot please God" [Romans 8:7-8]. In addition, we are to "love the Lord your God with all your heart, with all your soul, with all your strength, and with all your mind" [Luke 10:27]; with such a comprehensive command, when we fail, is there nothing "extra" we could ever do "to make up" for that failure? If a new-born needs the Savior, then *our* condition is that much more frightening.

"He who believes and is Baptized will be saved" [Mark 16:6] has been used by some to discourage infant baptism on the grounds that newborns cannot have faith. But if that is true, then the rest of the verse, "but he who does not believe will be condemned," would deny the same child any hope of salvation.[31] If newborns cannot have faith in the Savior, then they cannot have the "righteousness of God" – that perfection which allows us to stand before Jehovah's throne, which comes *"through faith* in Jesus Christ, to all and upon all *who believe"* [Romans 3:22], "the righteousness of God which is *of faith, through faith in Christ*" [Philippians 3:9]; and "the Scripture has imprisoned all under sin so that the promise *by faith* in Jesus Christ might be *given to those who believe*" [Galatians 3:22] – this requirement for salvation depends upon the individual's personal faith.

Without this righteousness, no class of human can enter heaven even based on *their own blamelessness.* Surprisingly, the Bible does speak of people who are "blameless": when Paul lists his pedigree in Philippians 3:4-6, he caps it off with, "concerning the righteousness which is in the law, *blameless*" (and this follows how he "persecuted the church" and brought suffering and death to the early believers!); John the Baptist's parents, Zachariah and Elizabeth, also are "blameless" [Luke 1:5-6]; and *Jehovah Himself* calls Job "blameless and upright" [Job 1:8]. The young man of Matthew 19:16-20 states that "from his youth" he has kept the list of commandments which Jesus identifies. Yet though "blameless," every one still falls under the judgment, "for *all* have sinned and fall short of the Glory of God" [Romans 3:23]. There is no one innocent and "blameless" enough to not have a profound need for faith in the Savior.

Sin in the Young Child

Sin is not merely something "wrong" – it is rebellion; it is to be aware of the "right" and yet deliberately go one's own way; it is selfishness which rules one's heart; it is a disregard for others in favor of one's own desires.

Do we see these things even in a young child? Yes, indeed, complete with temper tantrums. It does not matter that it may be a "stage" of growth; it does not matter that it lacks the sophisticated sin of the adult; it does not matter that the child may not fully understand what he is doing – it is still sin. It does not matter whether we have grown so used to such demonstrations that we even have a place for it in the psychology of the growing child. It does not mean that maturity could not be achieved in any other way. It does not mean that the Creator could not imagine anything different from what we are used to. It does not mean that this is how He *designed* the human being, that is, to mark the childhood with rebellion. It does mean what St Paul wrote: "for *all* have sinned and fall short of God's Glory" [Romans 3:23], young and old, *all* are in desperate need.

Despite claims that rebellion is "normal," as parents we recognize the need to guide the child away from sin. We encourage him to be sorry, to repent, to apologize to an offended person (usually another child). We want the child to know that we forgive him and so also does Jesus.

The Lord condemns all rebellion – there is not a breath in the Bible of excluding any age group. We plead in defense of the child that he may not have the capability to resist this sinfulness, which is true. However, as St Paul declares in Romans 7, neither do we as adults. We, as adults, look to the promised Holy Spirit to be the equipment we lack – a holy spiritual Presence in our lives, even where we do not always understand how He works in us. Why would our God not want to provide the still more helpless child this same equipment? Is there something which He would gain by withholding this blessing? Would refusing this help to a spiritually vulnerable child be expressing the same Love that would compel Him to go to the Cross?

The promise throughout the New Testament is that the Holy Spirit is bestowed in Baptism. This is the added spiritual equipment *needed* as the child forms his concepts of sin, forgiveness, repentance; as he learns to resist evil which he cannot do by his own ability; and by which he is guided as he discovers his Creator, his Savior, and his Helper, and, as possible in no other way, explores a personal relationship with his God.

Human Inventions vs Divine Gifts

"The Age of Accountability"

At what age can a child be recognized has having faith? If he is incapable of faith until some "age of accountability," then Jesus cannot be applied directly to his life. The child is left out of all benefits and blessings, out of any God-desired intimacy, and out of all the results which the Bible emphasizes come only through faith in Jesus – His forgiveness, Christ's indwelling, and the Spirit's indwelling, for example.

Yet there is no *Biblical* standard for any such "age of accountability." The distinction is entirely man-made and artificial, and we face the rather harsh comment by Jesus, "In vain they worship Me, teaching as doctrines the commandments of men" [Matthew 15:9]. The margin of error in this "doctrine" is too large: suppose we decide that a six-year-old may have faith, but a one-and-a-half-year-old cannot – but what if the reality is that a one-and-a-half-year-old *can* have faith? How would we know, especially when even in adults we have no way to measure what only the Holy Spirit can see for certain? This is something that has eternal consequence – we cannot afford to make mistakes here!

Child Dedication

"Child Dedication" as a replacement for infant Baptism is similarly problematic. Although there are many commands to Baptize and there are many references to Baptism and the relationship which it establishes, there is not one comparable word in regard to "Dedication." It is not commanded as a general treatment for children nor are there references to it concerning any specific spiritual benefits.

Yes, there are examples of a child being dedicated to the Lord, particularly Samuel [I Samuel 1: 27-28]. There is also:

> Consecrate to Me all the first-born; the first who opens the womb in all the people of Israel, both of man and of beast, he is Mine ... It was when Pharaoh hardened his heart and refused to let us go, Jehovah killed all the first-born in the land of Egypt, both the first-born of man to the first-born of beast. Therefore I sacrifice to Jehovah all the males who open the womb; *but all the first-born of my sons I redeem.* Exodus 13:2,15

Here the Lord indicates that since He preserved the lives of both human *and beast male firstborn* in the Passover in Egypt, that they belong to Him. This is no voluntary "dedicating," but *the surrendering of man and beast as commanded, and ransoming back the child!* And this only refers to the son who "opens" the womb, not to any other child. So when Jesus is presented in the Temple, Luke carefully informs the reader as to why [Luke 2:23].

So what about Samuel, and the children whom Jesus wants to come to Him [Matthew 19:14; Mark 10:14; Luke 18:16]? What is overlooked is that these children are already in Covenant relationship with Jehovah through Circumcision. They are not initiating a relationship, but rather operating within a personal connection they already have, which has become even more direct through Jesus' own Circumcision. And it must be repeated that Covenant is a relationship not of law, but of Love, of the joining of Blood/ Life/Soul. It is within this context that the children are invited into the blessings of the Lord.

The Groundwork of Circumcision

Some have wanted to dismiss the Old Testament as useless in our New Testament age, which is like saying the Jehovah of the Old Testament no longer exists and has been replaced. That is an awkward position, because God is unchangeable and eternal [Malachi 3:6; James 1:17; Revelation 1:8] –

the Old Testament is as much the history and diary of God's heart as the New Testament is. Circumcision in the Old Testament has important things to tell us about the Lord of Baptism.

In the Bible's very first book, Circumcision occurs in a pronounced environment of grace. Abraham lives thirteen years or so between Genesis 15, when Jehovah commits Himself in Covenant, and chapter 17, when this human now commits himself in Circumcision. The time span does not justify the idea that Baptism can wait that long, because now in chapter 17 when Circumcision is performed, the command is that *every* eight-day-old male infant must be included in this Covenant. However these years do indicate that Jehovah's Covenant is thoroughly grounded in His Glory: His mercy, grace, Steadfast Love, faithfulness, forgiveness and justice.

Trained over two thousand years, in every generation the Covenant People never ask about faith in the infant – they automatically include their eight-day-old son under Covenant because this is what Jehovah wants. Even today, now four thousand years later, the modern Jew – even the non-practicing Jew – still places his child under Covenant. Whatever else God may require, it is His responsibility to see that whatever Covenant requires is given to the individual, since there is no other way anyone could have such things.

To this day a Jew, even a not-so-good one, diligently circumcises his sons on the eighth day, because of the Covenant-command. It is so ingrained that it explains why the early Church was silent about infant-baptism. Originally the Church consisted entirely of Jews who accepted Jesus as the Messiah (*"Yeshuah Hammasheach"*) and who would naturally see baptizing their infants as entering them into the New Covenant. As membership became non-Jewish, distanced from Jewish thinking, the question grew, "Can an infant believe?"

For the Jew, this was immaterial, since *Yahweh El Shaddai*, Jehovah the Almighty God, reached down to include him into Covenant. Whether his infant understood made little difference – Jehovah did it. As his son grew, then it was necessary to teach him what being under Covenant meant. Surely, many "circumcised" did not live worthy of

Covenant, but broke it. Many prophets pleaded with this unique People (Israel) to have "a Circumcision of the heart" – a spiritual participation and entering into Covenant, beyond the physical marking. But that still did not make God change His mind and later require only adults to become circumcised. Rather, whenever there was faith, the LORD poured out the fullness of Covenant; whenever Covenant was defied, He separated Himself from the man or people.   Robert F. Lindemann[32]

Therefore when Peter proclaims, "For the promise is unto you and to your children" [Acts 2:39], it is a totally automatic reaction for his Jewish listeners to place their children under this "New Covenant." For something so ingrained over so many generations, there would be no need to command what is already so familiar.

What would cause confusion is the opposite, if this practice of including the eight-day-old infant is to cease. There would have to be many discussions in the Bible as to why this reversal in the attitude of Jehovah, why He would now specifically *exclude* infants.

These questions would be further aggravated by what this saved Jew himself would have heard taught in the New Testament time. For example, he would have heard Peter in his sermon on the Day of Pentecost, Acts 2: 38, 39: "Then Peter said unto them, 'Repent, and be Baptized every one of you in the name of Jesus Christ for the remission of sins, and ye shall receive the gift of the Holy Ghost. For the promise is unto you and to your children, and to all that are afar off, even as many as the LORD our God shall call.'" Remember, Peter said this to Jews, Jews who were used to having the outward sign of their faith applied to their children.

With all these things in his mind, he would expect his child to be Baptized. If it were refused, what would you have done in his place? You would have asked the Apostles the reason why. So would the thousands of Christian Jews in that day. The question would have been asked in a hundred meetings; and Peter, John, Paul, and the others would have sat down and written in their Epistles to clear up the matter, just as they answered other questions that arose. The New Testament would have contained the clear answer as to why in the Old Testament the Covenant sign was applied to the infants of believers, but in the New Testament it was to be withheld from them.

The only reason possible for the New Testament not dealing with this problem is that the problem did not exist. The only possible reason that there was no problem in the Jews' minds was that the believing Jews did apply the covenant sign to their children. They Baptized their babies as they had circumcised them in the Old Testament dispensation.

Francis A. Schaeffer[33]

As always, it is the Glory of God to have mercy, grace, goodness *and* Covenant, Whose heart's desire does not change because of a Covenant change – if anything, if possible, it has only heightened.

"For It Is God Who Works" [Philippians 2:13]

The Faith in a Newborn

The fact that children are used as a model for us to emulate [Luke 18:16,17; Matthew 18:3-4; Matthew 19:14] does not mean that they represent perfection. The emphasis is not on *"perfection"* but rather on *the absolute trust* that an infant has – after all, Jesus is calling the adults to *faith*, not self-righteousness. The irony is that as Jesus says to adults that they must have faith like the little child's, *some* turn to the child and tell him that his faith must be more *adult*-like if he is going to be acceptable to God. Who has the greater authority here?

Although the infant may not be as *conscious* of the operation of faith as the adult, it does not diminish the fact that he already has trust and dependence on those of whom he may have only meager awareness. When he cries in whatever the distress he may have – hunger, wet diaper, sleepiness, sickness – he expects that somebody will be there to answer the need. His sense of well-being and survival depends upon the parent's attention and involvement, as well as the comfort and security in being held close. Is not "dependency" in this case another way of saying "faith"?

A lack of sophistication is not the same as a lack of trust. It is precisely the simplicity and fundamental nature of the young child's faith which Jesus uses as the model for our faith in Jehovah. But even here, though the infant does trust on a human level, faith *in the Lord* must still be the Holy Spirit's gift and miracle – just as much for the infant as for the adult.

Baptism and Faith in Colossians[34]

> In Whom also you were circumcised with a Circumcision not made by hands, in the casting off the body of the sins of the flesh, in the Circumcision of Christ, co-buried with Him in Baptism, in Whom you were also raised through faith in the working of God, Who raised Him from the dead. Colossians 2:11-12

What is intriguing is that St Paul does not here mention "faith" in regard to Circumcision, nor in regard to "buried with Him in Baptism," but only in the section dealing with being "raised with Him" is it now brought in. Remember that Circumcision is a passive event – the infant does not, could not do it to himself. Baptism is also a passive event: it is never 'I Baptize myself,' but rather 'I am Baptized' by the hand of another: "I need to *be Baptized*" [Matthew 3:14]; "you shall *be Baptized*" [Acts 1:5]; "Arise and *be Baptized*" [Acts 22:16].

In the passage above, "you were circumcised … *in the Circumcision of Christ*," "you were … co-buried," "you also were raised" are all passive and even when faith shows up, it is "faith *in the working of God*, Who raised Him from the dead." It certainly does not sound as though faith makes all this happen, but rather it receives what has been done by God, it is holding on to the Promise found in God's raising Christ from the dead. It drives us back to the definition of the Glory of God found in Exodus 33:19, as Paul emphasizes to the Romans [9:15-16]:

For He says to Moses, "I will have mercy on whom I have mercy, and I will have compassion on whom I have compassion." So therefore, it depends not on him who is willing, nor on him who is striving, but on Him Who is showing mercy – God.

Jehovah acts because He chooses to, He wants to, He said He would. Our confession of faith may be defective, our fervency may be for all the wrong reasons, our understanding may be limited, our commitment may wax and wane over the years, our emotions may even run contrary to our faith – or be lacking at the moment, if not today, then perhaps tomorrow. But entrance into God's Covenant is not by negotiation – if it depends on us, indeed, "Who then can be saved?" We must come to terms with the realization that Jehovah acts according to His mercy and what He can do cannot be defined nor limited by our ability to understand:

> A faithful, God-fearing heart does this: it asks first whether it is God's Word. When it hears that it is, it smothers with hands and feet the question why it is useful or necessary. For it says with fear and humility, "My dear God, I am blind; truly I know not what is useful or necessary for me, nor do I wish to know, but I believe and trust that Thou dost know best and dost intend the best in Thy divine goodness and wisdom. I am satisfied and happy to hear Thy simple Word and perceive Thy will."   Martin Luther[35]

The joyful thing about rejecting the fear of Baptizing an infant is that even though we may finally have to admit that a new-born is thoroughly laced with sin, we do not have to resign it to that fate! Its Savior is right at hand! Instead of fighting the Bible's description of our natures as sinful from conception, why not spring right into the Glory and praise of the Savior Who has the immediate remedy right here, in something as simple as "the Water and the Word"!

And consider: by denying someone God's grace (a Sacrament), then are we not also denying (hindering [Acts 10:47; 11:17][36]) *God Himself* from a relationship *He* desires and from the pouring out His gifts in the way *He* said He would?

108

6. The Body of Christ *(See pages 23-26)*

Returning to "the Image"

The Unity Within "Christ"

"In that day you will know that I am in My Father, and you in Me, and I in you" [John 14:20] – in Jesus is that perfect connection between Jehovah and humans, and we must be "in Him" to have this relationship with God. By Baptism, we enter into one of St Paul's most powerful word images, "the Body of Christ," and it is a very strong image:

> "Body of Christ" is an extraordinary expression. It is without parallel even in the Old Testament. Seneca, to be sure, was quite ready to refer to the citizens of Rome as a body politic. We are quite familiar with terms "student body" or "church body." To speak of church members as a body of Christians creates no particular excitement. However, that is not what the apostle chose to write. He spoke of Christians as the "body of Christ." That is to say, in some mysterious sense the church is an extension of the incarnation of our Lord. It does His work. It is His instrument within history to carry on Christ's mission of gathering all things under His lordship. Martin H Scharlemann[37]

As one reads Paul's discussion concerning the Body of Christ in I Corinthians, there is a powerful Covenant – New Covenant – sense:

> For exactly as the [human] body is one and has many members, and all the members of the body, being many, are one body, likewise it also is with Christ. For in one Spirit we all were Baptized into one Body – whether Jews or Greeks, whether slaves or free men – and all were caused to drink of one Spirit. I Corinthians 12:12-13

"likewise it also is with Christ" – note that it is not "Christ *and* ... (the Church, or believers, or ...)" but simply, "Christ." Just as the mingled Blood in Covenant declares that it is the same life, the same Soul – the same *person* – that flows between Covenant partners, so also in Paul's mind there is a seamless indivisible unity in this Body. It is not merely an association of Jesus and the Church – "Christ" no longer, forever, just refers to Jesus alone, but rather simultaneously to Jesus, Head of the Body, *and us, His Body,* as one organic whole, so that even on the throne of heaven, wherever One is, the other *must* inseparably be:

> God … made us alive *with Christ* – by grace you are being saved – and "jointly raised up" and "jointly seated" us in the heavenly places *in Christ Jesus.* Ephesians 2:4-7 (Note: this is a *completed,* not future, action)

This is the reality behind being *Baptized into Christ* [Romans 6:3; Galatians 3:27], the reality behind Paul's constant use of "*in Christ*" – the actual oneness of Covenant:

> Consequently, the word "in" in the Colossians [2:9, 10] passage means far more than being in the same place as Christ, or being near Him, or He being near us. It means more than a partnership with Christ or Christ being a partner with us. It means that out of the two of us there is one new man. Christ is that man and I am in Christ to be that man.
> Theodore H. Epp[38]

What an eye-opener to read through Paul's letters in the New Testament with that reality behind the word "Christ"! The impression is that, first, God really is not casual about this; and, second, we really are a part of all this.

> We are not surprised that [*Jesus*] is exalted and enthroned in the heavens. What is difficult for us to comprehend is that *we* have been exalted with Him. Yet if "he that is joined unto the Lord is one spirit" (1 Cor 6:17), it cannot be otherwise. We are not surprised that "all things have been put under *His* feet." What we have failed to comprehend is that as a part of Him, His Body, all things are also legally beneath *our* feet. What we do not realize is that He is "the Head over all things *for the Church*" (Eph 1:22). This means that *His Headship over all things is assumed and held for the* **benefit of the Church** and is directed toward His purpose for her. We have underestimated the supreme importance of the Church in God's economy. *She is the center and motive of all His activity from all eternity.* He does nothing solely for His own sake. She is included as a full

partner in all His plans. The Church is His Body, the fullness of Him that fills all things everywhere. *He is not full or complete without His Church which is His Body.* Paul E. Billheimer[39]

Because all this *is* true, our amazement grows. We begin to realize how the Father would treat us just like He would His Son, with exactly the same status as His Son – because we truly *are* the Body of Christ.

Surpassing Adam's Mission

So it has been written, "The first man Adam became a living Soul." The last Adam became a Life–giving Spirit. I Corinthians 15:45

Mankind is created to be "the Image of God," in the Blood-likeness, or Soul-likeness of the Creator. Of course, after the Fall, rather than reflecting Jehovah's heart and Soul, instead the human heart has been filled only with the chaos of rebellion.

But now in Baptism, becoming the Body of Christ and "participating in divinity" as discussed earlier – there is something radically different here: no longer are we to just reflect "the Image of God," we have become the actual extension of Jesus' incarnation. We are His heart, His voice, His hands, His presence (living *in* us) in this world. Now on the throne of heaven, Jesus equips us to even surpass *His* revelation of God when He walked this earth:

Very truly, I say to you, he who believes in Me, the works which I do he will do, and greater works than these he will do, because I go to My Father. John 14:12

"To those who believe, these signs will follow – in My Name: they will cast out demons; they will speak with new tongues; they will take up snakes; and if they drink anything deadly, in no way will it hurt them; they will lay hands on the sick, and they will have health."

So then, after speaking to them, the Lord Jesus was taken up into heaven, and sat down at the right hand of God. They went out and preached everywhere, the Lord working with them and confirming the Word through the accompanying signs. Amen. Mark 16:17-20

[Peter] found there a certain man, Aeneas by name, who was paralyzed and for eight years was lying on a mattress. Peter said to him, "Aeneas, Jesus the Christ heals you. Arise and make your bed." Immediately he arose. So all who lived in Lydda and Sharon saw him and turned to the Lord.   Acts 9:33-35

What extraordinary privilege! Perhaps most puzzling in all this is how Jesus will do nothing in regard to many things but especially in regard to the world's salvation, except through His Body – through the hands of these humans. Could we ever understand how the Creator of the Universe, He Who suffered to death for the sake of the lost, how *He* would so *utterly* depend on *us?* And yet His wisdom is that we, as members of His Body are never meant to be useless appendages. We think that living as Christ's Body is of optional importance, but in a surprising but characteristic humility, Jesus makes *us* of utmost necessity.

We are Highly Valued

Eastern Religions

God's high opinion of us is in extreme contrast to eastern religions (Hinduism, Buddhism, and others). Their concept of "God" is that He is a non-Person, variously described as "the great ocean of life," "the ground of all being."[40] Although this is over-simplifying, the version of "sin" in this framework is when a "portion" of this "great ocean of life" separates itself from the rest and becomes *an individual.* Therefore the end goal of these religions, through meditation, reincarnation, and so forth, is to empty oneself, to lose oneself, to cease being an individual, and finally to be reabsorbed in the "ground of all being."

The basic message is that one is a nothing and has no really important role to fulfill. Who cares what one's talents and abilities are – they are meaningless anyway. In fact, the human is ultimately meaningless.

Evolution

Should it be a surprise that evolution has the same message? Although we like to talk about the upward climb of evolution, a true evolutionist could never speak that way. Its conjectured process is totally random, and what survives may not be a "better" organism, or the one best adapted to all environments. The final endpoint of evolution is either "the Big Crunch" when the universe collapses in upon itself, or where there is just not enough "mass" to slow down its expansion, and so on it goes to finally simply run out of useable energy.

This philosophical base (it *is* a philosophy, rather than a science) is very attractive, because it starts with the idea that there is no God, there is no one paying attention to what we do. It means that we can do whatever we want to do and we are accountable to nobody. Our human nature just loves this idea, and it should be no surprise that it has such popularity, even to strident and belligerent support.

But the "teeth" to this philosophy is in its conclusions: It may be so comforting that no one is paying attention to us, but on the other hand, *no one is paying attention to us*. Ultimately no one cares about us. We don't matter at all *to anything*. When the universe ends either way, there will be no one to even say that it was worth the journey. No one will be there to note our greatest accomplishments, neither as an individual, nor as a nation, nor as a race of beings, nor as the product of evolution. Everything ultimately ends up as nothing: our day is nothing; as we look back on what we did, it is nothing; any progress we may think we achieved is nothing.

Ironically the great cry is how people today have low self-esteem, yet is it any wonder when this growing philosophical base of our culture constantly concludes that we really are not worth anything anyway? In fact, the human is ultimately meaningless.

Present and Eternal Value

What a very rich opposite to such philosophies is "the Body of Christ"! We are indeed part of something far greater than just ourselves and we are *not* nothings! "Individuals" within the Body are not abhorred but rather are treasured for the unique combination of talent and ability which each brings.

Just as the individual parts of our body *must* be different from the rest – the heart cannot do kidney functions, nor do we want the liver trying to be a bone –, so also within the Body of Christ our need for *each individual* is intensified. The whole Body benefits precisely because of what each member has and is – each person contributes something that no one else can. And since we, Christ's Body, are seated on the throne of heaven with Him, then this importance and usefulness extends into eternity.

Back around 1900, the "scientific" world identified over 180 items in the human body as "vestigial" – unnecessary leftovers and dead ends from evolution. Over the years, as more has been learned about the human body, that number has eventually shrunk to "0" – nothing is useless tissue, everything has a role to play in the various functions of the body. Even the appendix contributes to the digestion, the immunology, the growth, and the endocrine systems.

In a world crying out for "self-esteem," what a powerful and eternal answer "the Body of Christ" provides! Everybody is essential. What a wonderful awareness with which to surround children as they grow up: they are valuable and useful – the Body of Christ *needs* them, *even right now ("as a little child," Jesus had said).* Moreover, they are connected to the Body of the living, vibrant Christ of all ages for their support, help, and strength throughout their lives.

> until we all arrive at the unity of the faith and of the knowledge of God's Son; into a "finished" Man; into the measure of the stature of Christ's fullness, ... speaking the truth in Love may we grow into Him in all ways, Him Who is the Head, Christ, from Whom the whole Body, fitted together and joined together by what every joint supplies, when each part is working properly, makes bodily growth and upbuilds itself in Love. Ephesians 4:13-16

Diversity

Varieties of Gifts, Service, Working

> There are diversities of gifts, but the same Spirit; there are diversities of ministries, but the same Lord; there are diversities of works, but the same God Who works all things in all – to each is given the manifestation of the Spirit for the common good.
>
> To one is given through the Spirit the word of wisdom, and to another the word of knowledge according to the same Spirit, to a different one faith in the same Spirit, to another gifts of healing in the one Spirit, to another the working of power, to another prophecy, to another the discerning of spirits, to a different one various kinds of tongues, to another the interpretation of tongues. All these are worked by the one and the same Spirit, who distributes to each one individually as he wills. I Corinthians 12:4-11

Based upon the quote's first paragraph, the suspicion is that the listing in the second paragraph is really just the tip of the iceberg in regard to all the ways that the Spirit "manifests" Himself within the Body of Christ. What is so extraordinary about Paul's vision of the Body of Christ, first of all, is its concrete reality to him, but also that the differences in the People of God are by deliberate design, just as with the human body.

Each part is unique, having a special job that the rest of the Body cannot do. The grasp of the hand cannot be duplicated anywhere else on the Body. The ability to hear, to speak, to see, to taste, to pump the Blood, to bring a breath of fresh air into the Body, to run, to… are all abilities unique to distinctive parts or combination of parts within the body. What value and importance God has placed upon each individual member of the body! That in itself provides strong encouragement to each individual in Christ's Body to not only recognize one's own value and meaning, but also "that there may be no schism/discord in the Body, but that the members may have the same care for one another" [v 25].

Often we seem to expect that the Body should be one big shapeless, indistinguishable lump, usually based on where our own interests and abilities lie. If others should not do what we can do well, if they should not see and understand and react in "the right way" (our way), we then tend to look down upon them, their spirituality or their commitment. Or else we feel intimidated because we do not do the same things (prayer, evangelism, verse memorization, and so much more) as well as others. But Jesus never designed His people to be a shapeless one-task Body!

> If the foot said, "Because I am not a hand, I am not part of the body," for this reason would it not be part of the body? If the ear said, "Because I am not an eye, I am not of the body," for this reason would it not be a part of the body? If the whole body were an eye, where is the hearing? If the whole body were hearing, where is the sense of smell?
> I Corinthians 12:15-17

Despite where one part of the Body may not understand what, how, and perhaps even why another part does what it does, when the Church comes to grips with the reality that the differences are by *God's* design, then something wonderful can happen. Unfortunately, it often may take some sort of tragedy to finally bring this realization. Then, at least for the moment, the different abilities and gifts surface, and the Body of Christ lives and acts according to God's blueprint.

> Indeed He gave some to be apostles, some prophets, some evangelists, and some shepherds and teachers, towards the perfecting of the saints into the work of ministry, into building up Christ's Body, until we all arrive at the unity of the faith and of the knowledge of God's Son; into a "finished" Man; into the measure of the stature of Christ's fullness
> Ephesians 4:11-13

> For He is our peace, Who has made both [Jew and Gentile] one ..., so that from the two He would create in Himself one new man, thus making peace, that He might reconcile them both to God in one Body through the Cross ... because through Him we both have access by one Spirit to the Father. Ephesians 2:14-16, 18

Sadly, when the crisis is over, everybody too often returns to business as was usual. But, when a Church grabs ahold of this concept of the unity in diversity, when every individual is treasured for his unique combination of gifts/abilities – what a wonderful vision of God at work this presents. When Jesus is truly unleashed through the many gifts and talents of His Body, what amazing and powerful things could He do? Then St Paul is discovered as really knowing what he is talking about when he says, "when each part is working properly, [this] makes bodily growth and upbuilds itself in Love" [Ephesians 4:16].

Whose Body?

> The branch has to bear fruit, but if the branch imagines that it is going to produce a cluster or even a grape by itself, it is utterly mistaken. The fruit of the branch comes through the stem. Your work for Christ must be Christ's work in you or else it will be good for nothing.... Beware of homemade schemes. Do for Jesus what Jesus bids you do. Remember that our work for Christ – as we call it – must be Christ's work first if it is to be accepted of Him. Abide in Him as to your fruitbearing.
> Charles Spurgeon[41]

Ultimately, this is *Christ*'s Body. Therefore when each part does the unique job given to it, it is expressing Christ Himself's presence and activity – *each* is Jesus' living proof that He is in the midst of His People! Hear the voice of the Beloved through him who is Christ's tongue; discern God's activity through the insight of her who is Christ's eyes; experience God's steadfast Love especially through him who is Christ's heart; lean on the quiet strength and encouragement through her who is the "bones" of Jesus.

God intended that no one, other than Jesus, would do "all things well" and we cannot be everywhere, doing everything at the same time. In fact, Jesus chooses to *not* do all things well by Himself without His Body. What patience He must have with us, while He waits for us to catch on as to what we are about. He has compelled us to need each other, to value each other, to depend on each other, to learn from each other, and to grow with each other.

The Care for Every Member – Large and Small

Even the Little Toe

We make the effort to take good care of our body, feeding it, clothing it, washing it, etc. Would Jesus do any less for His Body? Perhaps this is part of the significance of Jesus' washing the feet of His disciples [John 13:1-17].

We also care a great deal when a part of our own body hurts in some way. Even one of the smallest members, the little toe, although farthest from the head, is very important to us. If we stub it, the whole body bends over in pain, the whole body walks with a limp. If it has a serious infection, the whole body can run a fever. People who have had their little toes amputated find that even many years later their senses of balance and of direction are still affected.

So the smallest and seemingly most insignificant member of the body is greatly valuable and necessary to the body! Every one of us – you, me, the infant being Baptized – is vitally important to Jesus, often despite the insignificance the world places upon various individuals. If we hurt, *He* hurts; if we are honored, *He* rejoices; His care for us is the same as care for His Body – *because we* **are** *that Body!* God Himself wants this kind of assured connection, and this is the comfort and security into which we place the Baptized – adult and child.

And how wonderful it is to *know* He will help – according to His wisdom as seen in Creation, according to his Steadfast Love as seen on the Cross, according to His power as seen in His Resurrection. No one is too small or insignificant in Christ's Body!

Reciprocal Resources and Reserves

A properly functioning Body of Christ has so much to offer each member by way of resources and mutual strength – what self-help groups such as Alcoholics Anonymous and Weight Watchers have only "recently" discovered, has been available in the Church for millennia! The strength of these groups is that they are united and open about the needs that they have and welcome all who wish to participate in this community. The Body of Christ also has always been, among other things, the gathering of those in need. We also come with a problem which we have in common, the rebellion of sin that affects our lives. Perhaps every speaker at a Church meeting should introduce himself as "Hi, my name is (Jim) and I am a sinner. I have been under God's mercy and grace for (over sixty) years" as in the Alcoholics Anonymous program. Perhaps that humility might moderate some of the difficult feelings into which church meetings may get themselves.

And not to be forgotten, the Body of Christ always has an extra: the resources found within aren't just *human* – they are *God's* resources, of the special combination of God and Man that is Jesus:

> For we have a High Priest, not one who is unable to suffer with us in our weaknesses, but One Who has been tested in all things just like we are, yet without sin – therefore we should with confidence approach the Throne of Grace, that we may receive mercy and find grace for timely help.... let us approach with a true heart in full confidence of faith, the hearts being sprinkled from an evil conscience and the bodies washed with pure water. Hebrews 4:15-16; 10:22

As surely as our bodies are connected to our heads and share all things in common (good and bad), so it is with Christ and His Body – we have access to all the forgiveness, patience, power, Love, and everything else that Jesus has, especially when ours runs dry.

He Depends on US

> Here your heart must go out in love and learn that this is a sacrament of love. As love and support are given to you, you in turn render love and support to Christ in His needy ones. Some gladly share the profits but not the costs – they like to hear that in this sacrament the help, fellowship, support of all the saints are promised and given to them. But they are unwilling in turn to give themselves into this fellowship – they won't help the poor, suffer with the suffering, put up with sinners, intercede for others, care for the sorrowing, defend the truth, and at risk of their own life, property, and honor seek the betterment of the Church and of all Christians ... They are self-seeking, and this sacrament does not benefit them! Martin Luther[42]

There is obligation here! A non-functioning member cripples the Body ("I will go but I do not want to join"), and a perfectly good member who amputates itself ("I do not feel I need church") kills itself and harms the rest of the Body. In all the Bible, there is no such thing as a "spiritual hermit" – a person who is disconnected from the rest of the spiritual community! The

Vine does not bear fruit unless "the branches" – we – are participants in His action: the dependence on us to which God has committed Himself, without reservation, and without alternate plan is staggering and humbling.

> This great truth was put to me very simply years ago, "God has a plan. You have a part. Find it. Follow it." How wonderful that each of us can have a part in carrying out God's plan. Unless we learn to listen for the guidance of His Holy Spirit and obey Him, we will miss our part.
> Possibly that is what is wrong with the world. So many people miss their parts. Either through indifference or unbelief, or just plain disobedience. That is the reason why prayer is so vitally important. It helps the people for whom we pray find God's way and their part in it. It also helps us to find God's way and our part in it.
>
> Helen Smith Shoemaker

How important it is to help each other, especially our children, be fully functioning members of Christ's Body, so that each CAN rely *upon the Body* and *upon Christ* for what he needs in his life with the Lord, and *give* of himself to help build up and strengthen Christ's Body.

> For Christ was born to bear other Christs. Christmas is meaningless unless it means not merely God-in-a-stable but God-in-a-person, God in you. Christmas means grace, and grace means that you are Christ-bearers, Christophers in the richest meaning of the word: "It is no longer I who live, but Christ who lives in me" (St Paul to the Galatians 2:20). And not merely in me: with the coming of Christ, God has come to live in and with a people, a community of faith and hope and love.
>
> Walter J. Burghardt[43]

The Power of the Church

The Church and Baptism

> In contradiction to what has been said, some might cite the baptism of infants who do not comprehend the promise of God and cannot have the faith of baptism; so that therefore either faith is not necessary or else infant baptism is without effect. Here I say what all say: Infants are aided by the faith of others, namely, those who bring them for baptism.

For the Word of God is powerful enough, when uttered, to change even a godless heart, which is no less unresponsive and helpless than any infant. So *through the prayer of the believing church which presents it,* a prayer to which all things are possible [Mark 9:23], the infant is changed, cleansed, and renewed by inpoured faith. Nor should I doubt that even a godless adult could be changed, in any of the sacraments, *if the same church prayed for and presented him, as read of the paralytic in the Gospel, who was healed through the faith of others [Mark 2:3-12].* I should be ready to admit that in this sense the sacraments of the New Law are efficacious in conferring grace, not only to those who do not, but even to those who do most obstinately present an obstacle. *What obstacle cannot be removed by the faith of the church and the prayer of faith? Do we not believe that Stephen converted Paul the Apostle by this power? [Acts 7:58-8:1].* But then the sacraments do what they do not by their own power, but by the power of faith, without which they do nothing at all, as I have said.

Martin Luther[44] [Emphases mine]

What sometimes is overlooked is that the Church (the Eternal Church) is not a product of human ideas, but rather is the creation of Jesus Himself. The person who rejects the Church argues not with the humans but rather with its Lord. *Jesus* counts this community as essential, and it is much more than merely the sum of all its parts – after all it is the extension of our living Savior on this earth! As the resurrected Jesus breathed on His disciples, saying, "Receive the Holy Spirit: whomever's sins you forgive, they are forgiven to them; whomever's sins you retain, they are retained" [John 20:22-23], through them, through this bond, the Sacraments have their power. And it is within that power that the Holy Spirit will accomplish things which are beyond our understanding. How can *our* faith cause forgiveness and faith to enter a person's life? How can *our* prayers open another's life to the working of the Holy Spirit? God is not interested in explaining what we would not understand anyway. We must be content with the reality that He has chosen to work this way.

Non-Christian Baptizers

Sometimes a question arises as to whether a non-Christian (that is, Buddhist, atheist, Satanist) can Baptize someone who genuinely seeks this Sacrament. Some say yes, because as Luther points out, God's will and action is dependent on Himself, not on humans, despite what they may or may not believe.

> Whether even a wicked priest can minister at, and dispense, the Sacrament ... For here we conclude and say: Even though a knave takes or distributes the Sacrament, he receives the true Sacrament, that is, the true body and blood of Christ, just as truly as he who [receives or] administers it in the most worthy manner. For it is not founded upon the holiness of men, but upon the Word of God. And as no saint upon earth, yea, no angel in heaven, can make bread and wine to be the body and blood of Christ, so also can no one change or alter it, even though it be misused. For the Word by which it became a Sacrament and was instituted does not become false because of the person or his unbelief.
>
> Martin Luther[45]

However, Luther is speaking within the context of the Church, so does the above John 20 passage provide another aspect to this? Baptism falls under the same framework as the forgiving and the retaining of sins: "Repent, and be Baptized every one of you in the Name of Jesus Christ for the forgiveness of your sins ..." [Acts 2:38; see 22:16]; and "that He might sanctify her, having cleansed her by the washing of Water in the Word" [Ephesians 5:26]. Only the Church – and those who are part of it – have that authority to forgive sins in the Name of God, an action which is recognized in heaven.

It would seem then that those who are outside the group whom Jesus has specifically commissioned would not be empowered by the Holy Spirit. As well, in the Old Testament, Circumcision has the idea of the passing on of Covenant, by one already under Covenant, despite whether he was faithful or not – there is no idea given that merely anyone Circumcising anyone else automatically places them into Covenant.

Truly one may imagine different scenarios which we cannot answer in God's stead, so those we leave in His hands, and simply say that when there is opportunity, Baptism should be performed only by one who himself dwells within this Covenant.

7. *The Kingdom of God* (See pages 27-30)

What Citizenship Means

The relationship into which God sets us in Baptism is so rich and vast that no one picture will adequately describe it. Being a child of God and a member of Christ's Body are not two different relationships, but the same one from two different viewpoints. When Jesus tells us that "unless one is born again, he cannot see the Kingdom of God" [John 3:3], Baptism is here directly linked with citizenship in God's Kingdom and it provides yet another definition of this most amazing relationship designed for both God and us to enjoy.

Worldly citizenship is considered to be extremely important – to the point where all sorts of treaties guarantee that even the child born in international waters or on an international airplane flight will have some sort of citizenship immediately. The main reason is for protection, so that no person is alone, bur rather something a lot bigger and stronger than himself will be his champion should some country or group treat him improperly.

Citizenship is meant to defend the citizen and often to guarantee his rights. Some countries even allow challenges when the government has abused or infringed on these rights. However, there is also a balance here: although the individual's rights are to be protected, at the same time, *the country also has rights*. For example, it can call on its citizens for mutual defense (conscription), for taxation, and for exercising "good citizenship" (voting, volunteering, and other such support). Another important element is that each citizen is an ambassador of his country wherever he goes – the opinion of others concerning his country will depend on how he acts.[46]

Citizenship includes privileges. A child born in North America participates in its amazing wealth. Contrast the lack of food in some countries with the effort to sell day-old bread here. Or the educational opportunities just not available in some parts of the world. Or the abundance of recreational choices which we take for granted, the ability to travel on good roads, the variety of foods, the energy resources – all this and more in which even our youngest children participate *simply by being born into this country*!

Heavenly Citizenship

Membership

> So then you are no longer foreigners and aliens, but you are fellow citizens of the saints and of the household of God.   Ephesians 2:19

> Who delivered us out from the dominion of darkness and transferred us into the Kingdom of His beloved Son.   Colossians 1:13

We are placed into God's Kingdom and have citizenship under Jehovah's rule. Heavenly citizenship has direct parallels to the earthly variety. By spiritual birth, one becomes the recipient of all sorts of guaranteed rights, responsibilities, and privileges under the Lord's rule.

Heavenly Rights

The responsibility of every country is to guard and protect its citizens. The King of the Universe can call out His "Armed Forces" – His holy angels – for the sake of His People, some examples being: Elisha's protection [II Kings 6:13-18]; the legions of angels at the King's disposal [Psalm 68:17; Matthew 26:53]; and guardian angels [Matthew 18:10].

Since *Eternal Life* is involved, the strategy and goal may be a bit different than to merely preserve life on earth. Still, a great comfort is found in knowing that we do not face injustice and abuse alone – our King Himself experienced such indignity, and even turned His ordeal into the greatest blessing Creation has ever seen.

Canadians call it the "Charter of Freedoms," in the US it is the "Bill of Rights" – it is the guarantee to the citizenry that certain freedoms are not to be violated. So also even the King of the Universe has *His* "Charter of Freedoms" guaranteed to His citizens:

Freedom from Hopelessness	Romans 4:16-25
Freedom from God's Wrath	5:6-11
Freedom from Guilt (Judgment)	5:12-21
Freedom from Sin	6:1-23
Freedom from the Law (Condemned)	7:4-11
Freedom from Death	8:1-17
Freedom from Weakness	8:18-39

This "Charter of Freedoms'" overflowing fullness will reach its finale in OUR resurrection, as we enter full-fledged presence in His Kingdom.

Obviously, on this side of Heaven we do not experience the fullness of these freedoms. For example, we do presently have a certain freedom from sin and weakness, but not like what it will be when we finally enter into the full rights of the Kingdom on the Last Day. Yet that does not weaken the fact that these freedoms truly belong to us, endowed upon us by our King and they will be ours literally for eternity. Like the Promised Land for Israel, although it was given to Abraham, it was a while before the People could fully enjoy their ownership.

Privileges

Citizenship in God's Kingdom opens such opportunities for us: on earth, the happenstance of birth provides a vast wealth of privileges to a child born here, but imagine the universe-wide and eternity-wide wealth of privileges and opportunities which are available to one born into the Kingdom of God! Throughout the pages of the Bible, again and again we witness the Creator of the heavens and earth bending the powers and the resources of the universe and of His Kingdom for the sake of His People. Yet the greatest privilege is this:

> A happy Christian met an Irish peddler and exclaimed, "It's a grand thing to be saved!"
> "Aye," said the peddler, "It is, but I know something better than that."
> "Better than being saved?" asked the other. "What can you in your position possibly know that is better than that?"
> Came the reply, "The companionship of the Man Who saved me."[47]

Part of the mystery of God's Steadfast Love is His drive to be "Immanuel" – "God with us." In a world where the leaderships of nations and corporations are seemingly as remote as possible from their "little people," the royalty of this Kingdom delights in being with us. In fact, "Do you not know that you are the temple of God and the Spirit of God dwells in you?" [I Corinthians 3:16; also 6:19-20] This is no "theory," but rather the *Glory* of the Creator's personal and intimate involvement with every one of us, His beloved People.

Responsible Citizenship

All citizenship includes *give* as well as *take*. Although God can do all things by Himself, He *chooses* to work through *us – that we might share in the joy of his accomplishments!* He actually wants us to participate in the management of His Creation, a task to practice here so that we will be familiar with the job when we get to heaven.

Yet if we indeed are to represent Him throughout eternity, then we must reflect His characteristics. One such attribute is His servant nature, in accordance with which He is constantly giving, supporting, upholding. From the moment of creation, God has had to serve and to give in order to sustain life. The climax is where we discover that He withholds nothing for the sake of His Creation in the self-giving of Jesus, first at Christmas and then on the Cross. Yet that is not the end: Jesus continues to give Himself within His People and especially in Word and Sacrament. Moreover, the Holy Spirit has even volunteered to be a "live-in Servant," to do all those things inside us which we just cannot do.

We have seen His Steadfast Love in this type of giving; "For you know the grace of our Lord, Jesus Christ, that because of you, although being rich He became poor, so that you by His poverty might become rich" [II Corinthians 8:9]. As His citizens we seek the success of His Kingdom and it is foolish to think that this does not involve money; however, the motivation for this kind of giving must be the reflection of His Love: "they gave themselves first to the Lord and also to us, through the will of God" [v 5].

Our giving therefore reaches farther than money: we learn confidence and dependence on God as we look to His promises about taking care of us when we "seek first His Kingdom and His Righteousness" [Matthew 6:33]; we actually can have a part in the growth of our Lord's Kingdom here on earth; and we test the discipline of wise choices about our resources which do not depend on what is merely convenient.

More than mere citizens, we are His *ambassadors*, representing His nature to the *cosmos*, "God making His appeal through us" [II Corinthians 5:20-6:1] – we represent the King! How will others get to know Who and What He is except for how He is experienced through us? This is a very daring trust on His part – sometimes we are the only contact these people will have with the Kingdom. Their opinion – no, their eternity – can depend on how we have portrayed our Lord and His Glory.

This concept of being an ambassador had a particular emphasis in the Roman world of Jesus' day: as far as the empire was concerned, one was either a Roman citizen or a "barbarian." Romans were special and set apart. There were things that others might do and say to which a Roman would not stoop. He was different. Although he could not help but mingle with the "barbarians" in the streets, the Roman could still be identified at once by his conduct and attitude. His very bearing distinguished him from all others. So when St Paul tells the church in the Roman colony of Philippi in the midst of "barbarian" Greece, "But our citizenship is already in heaven, from which we await a Savior, the Lord Jesus Christ" [Philippians 3:20], they would instantly recognize that his message to them (and us) is that God's special citizens also have a certain dignity to which they bear witness before the world. Paul bids us to imitate him [v 17], as he longingly looks toward his homeland, while his whole bearing, conduct, manner, and even speech all reflect his vision of the joy and the Steadfast Love which he sees there.

However, the Philippians also realized that as a Roman colony "out on the frontier," they also had to be prepared to defend the empire against any threats. Throughout history, conscription (or "the draft") outside of wartime had as its basis the idea of a prepared and trained citizenry able to immediately raise a skilled army in defense of any attacks. St Peter urges us, the citizens of Heaven, to be similarly trained, not so much from physical as from verbal and spiritual attack – particularly when Satan seeks to weaken the importance of Jesus – "always being ready to give an answer to all who ask you to account for *the hope* which is in you" [I, 3:15].

Unfortunately most of us Christians do not realize that we have no time to lose – the battle has already been going on and we are ill-prepared. Nor do we believe how heavily the King is depending on His citizens in this fight. As in so many other areas of His earthly activity, although He does

130

not *need* us, still He has chosen to make us essential. When we submit to His training, He will use this opportunity to bring the heavy artillery of His Word and the Holy Spirit to bear on the people around us *through* us.

Of course, good citizens are involved in community life – the Kingdom's community life – because they truly want the Kingdom to succeed. They help maintain good leadership through responsible service and voting. They seek the proper community atmosphere for the maturing of the "young" citizens. They develop means for fellowship so that the community bond might be strengthened and enhanced, and available for times of celebration, disaster and need. They also use this time to celebrate the triumphs and the successes of their King.

Citizenship can be Lost

As with any "citizenship", through foolishness or neglect it can be lost -- although the King won't give up on us that easily. It can be thrown aside as if it were meaningless; it can even be renounced – often without realizing what one is giving up. Therefore, if it is important to teach our children the value and the responsibilities of *earthly* citizenship, how much more crucial is it to acquaint them with the value and the responsibilities of *heavenly* citizenship!

For parents there is comfort in knowing that God Himself has responsibility for the safety (especially the eternal safety) and welfare of their children, and they can claim the rights He has guaranteed each child-citizen.

The Kingdom of Priests

The Design

You shall be to Me a kingdom of priests and a holy nation…

Exodus 19:6

You also as living stones be built into a spiritual house, to be a holy priesthood, to offer spiritual sacrifices acceptable to God through Jesus Christ. ... But you are a chosen generation, a royal priesthood, a holy nation, a People purchased [by God], that you may proclaim the praises of Him Who called you out of darkness into His marvelous light

I Peter 2:5, 9

The Creator always intended that humanity would do more than just serve each individual self, but would have the extreme honor of being the priests of Creation, the ones who would present to the Lord the praises of this *cosmos*, and who would return, bringing His will and blessings to these creatures. An example of this task can be found in Psalm 148, where all Creation is called on to praise the Lord.

The rebellion of sin changed the landscape. Adam and Eve broke their connection not only with Jehovah, but also with Creation, and the universe has become adrift.

Old Testament Priesthood

Therefore you and your sons with you shall keep/heed your priesthood in every "word"/command concerning the altar and behind the veil; and you shall serve – I have given you the priesthood as a heritage of service, but the outsider who approaches [the altar] shall be put to death.

Numbers 18:7; also 16:40

No one takes this honor upon himself, but he who is called by God, just as Aaron was.　　　　　　　　　　　　　　　Hebrews 5:4

Jehovah never abandoned His intention. In Exodus 19, He stated that Israel would be "a nation of priests." However, the People made it clear as they wandered in the wilderness that they were too intent on their favorite pastime of complaining, griping, and rebelling for them to bother with such a high honor. They lost the privilege, which was then given to Aaron and his sons as "a heritage of service."

Such a high honor from God Himself was no casual thing! The Israelite priest was invested as the guardian for the People's connection with God, a position neither chosen nor earned but simply inherited. As a child he was a priest, although not yet practicing. He was to live distinctively because of who he was. As he grew older, he apprenticed and then finally assumed the duties of his station.

He was to ensure that the sacrifices which were given to Jehovah were the best: not the leftovers, the sick, the weak, the worn out, but only those animals in the fullness of life, without blemish or fault – as Jesus would be, as His People are to be [Ephesians 5:27]. After the worshipper confessed his sin on the head of God's chosen innocent victim (the animal which ultimately represented Jesus), the priest took its Blood, the Soul/Life forfeited by sin's rebellion, and poured it out before the Lord, signifying that the debt of sin was paid by this substitute and reassuring the worshipper of forgiveness.

Besides this *Sin Offering*, the priest also was in charge of the *Whole Burnt Offering* (demonstrating the whole commitment of the worshipper to Jehovah) and the *Peace Offering* (a communion between the Lord, the worshipper, and the priest who represented the community). Additionally there were the happier occasions of the People as represented by the *Thank Offerings*.

He also was in the role of intercessor, entrusted with the Altar of Incense, the symbol of the People's prayers, which he would bring before the Lord.

His position was not trivial. When Aaron's sons, Nadab and Abihu, did not respect the holiness of their function, they died [Leviticus 9:23-10:3]. The priests who took the Ark of the Covenant into battle against the Philistines (as if it were merely a good luck charm which required no heart-connection with Jehovah) died, and the Ark was captured [I Samuel 4:1-11]. God had commanded that the Ark was to be carried by poles on the shoulders of only the Levites, but when David was bringing the Ark to Jerusalem by ox-drawn cart, Uzzah (not a Levite) reached out to steady it and was struck dead [II Samuel 5:1-7]. Representing the Lord's holiness before His People was of considerable consequence and it required a heart of obedience.

The Liturgy

> I beseech you therefore, brethren, by the compassions of God, that you present your bodies as a living sacrifice, holy, well-pleasing to God, which is your logical service. Do not conform yourselves to this age but be transformed by the renewing of your mind, that you may confirm/reflect what is the will of God, what is good and acceptable and perfect.
> Romans 12:1-2

The High Priest Aaron had been only the harbinger of the one Man Who has brought this position to its climax: Jesus, the perfect High Priest and the perfect human. However, He simply will not hold this office without His Kingdom, His Bride, by His side – as His Body, He makes us God's sought-for "Nation of Priests." Through Baptism, this honor is a heritage by birth born "of Water and the Spirit," born as children of Jehovah Himself – He exalts His People into *Royal* Priests [I Peter 2:9 above].

No longer would the worship be the domain of a certain group. The early Church began to describe the work of Christians as a "Liturgy" (*leitourgia*) [II Corinthians 9:12; Acts 13:2], a Greek word which means "the work (*ergon*) of the people (*laos* – laity)." In ancient Greece, this concept spoke of what the people would do for the good of the whole community, whether it was to help build a public building, dig a well, create a statue for the public square, or to help in the political affairs.

134

Some might recognize "Liturgy" since it is applied to our common worship service. After all, in the joint confession of faith, the singing, the give-and-take of the responsive readings, and in other parts of service, the members are encouraging, strengthening, reminding, assuring, forgiving, and proclaiming to those who surround them, and so much more. It is indeed "the work of the people for the common good."

However as the Romans passage above implies, this "Priesthood of All Believers" encompasses a far larger domain than just what occurs in the "House of God." St Paul instructs us "whether you eat or drink, or whatever you do, do all to the glory of God" [I Corinthians 10:31], identifying in the verses surrounding this passage [23-33] that our "Liturgy" involves the effect on others of even seemingly mundane daily activities. In fact, what occurs in the Liturgy when the Church has gathered together ought to be the training ground for what we are, think, perceive, do and say out in the world.

> Here we practice – and live – our wonderful relationship with Jesus: we see Him fulfill His promises; we see Him give Himself totally to us; we see Him in those who surround us; we practice a lifestyle of His presence and of thanksgiving.
> When the service ends, none of this is over. Now we get to see how it works in our daily life. Now we test in deed what we learned, what we confessed, what we practiced. Gratitude and thanksgiving are the keynotes of our conduct, and the Bridegroom's joy seeps into our attitudes.   James Lindemann[48]

Unfortunately the idea of having Sunday School during the worship time has become popular. Instead, as priests "in training," the children should rather be where the Royal Priesthood is practicing its God-given function, so that they observe and grow in the work which marks their life at Jesus' side.

Our First Sacrifice

When Jesus died on the Cross, two things happened. The first was that the final and permanent sacrifice for sin had been accomplished – no sacrifice for sin can *we* do since only One can and has already done that. We are acceptable only because we are in Christ's Body and therefore participants in *His* "Offering and Sacrifice to God for a sweet–smelling aroma" [Ephesians 5:2].

> He has reconciled [you] in the Body of His flesh through death, to present you holy, and blameless, and without accusation in His sight.
> Colossians 1:22; also Ephesians 2:16

The second is that the veil in the temple, separating the common folk from the priesthood's activity was torn into two from top to bottom [Matthew 27:51]. Now all believers move into their God-desired role. But what are we now to do? As the Romans 12 passage above declares, our first responsibility is in regard to the sacrifice of ourselves – to become realigned with Jehovah in order to be part of the channel of praise and blessing which He desires.

Ours is the equivalent to *the Whole Burnt Offering*, the commitment of ourselves, our worlds and our walk of daily life wholly to the Lord. It is Bloodless since it is not our Life/Soul which God seeks, but Jesus' in us. There are two parts to this sacrifice we offer. The first is our bodies. Although the body, the flesh, is indeed the frustrating repository of sin [Romans 7:24], yet we are "bought at a price." By God's choice our body has become "the temple of the Holy Spirit Who is in you, Whom you have from God – you are not your own." Therefore we are to "Glorify God both in the spirit and *in the body*" [I Corinthians 6:19-20].

The body, controlled by the Old Nature, does have a will of its own [Romans 7:14-25], but part of our sacrifice is to "'pommel' my body and

136

subdue it" [I Corinthians 9:27], rather than giving in to its desires. This body is not to be used, for example, at the altar of sexual immorality, which "sins against one's own body" [I Corinthians 6:18]. Perhaps that is why Paul uses a strong Covenant contrast, "he who is joined to the Lord is one spirit with Him" [v 17], to remind us of the greater power we have in Jesus: "the body is... for the Lord, and the Lord for the body; and God both raised up the Lord and will raise us up by His power" [vv 13-14, 19].

This brings us to the other part of our sacrifice: "transformed by the renewing *of your mind.*" This means the humility of "a broken spirit, a broken and a contrite heart" [Psalm 51:17]; "through Him, we should offer up a sacrifice of praise in all things to God, that is, the fruit of lips which jointly profess His Name; do not neglect to do good and also to share" [Hebrews 13:15-16]; "To love Him with all the heart, with all the intellect, with all the Soul, and with all the strength, and to love one's neighbor as oneself, is more than all the [Old Testament] *Whole Burnt Offerings* and sacrifices" [Mark 12:33].

> ... there is the walk of the priesthood in harmony with its work. As God is holy, so the priest was to be especially holy. This means not only separated from everything unclean, but holy unto God – being set apart and given up to God for His use. Separation from the world and being given to God were indicated in many ways....
>
> In our separation from the world, we must prove that our desire to be holy to the Lord is whole-hearted and entire. The bodily perfection of the priest must have its counterpart in our also being "without spot or blemish." We must be "the man of God, perfect, thoroughly furnished unto all good works," "perfect and entire, wanting nothing" (Leviticus 21:17-21; Ephesians 5:27; 2 Timothy 3:17; James 1:4). ... We must forsake everything and like Christ have need only of God and keep everything for Him alone. This marks the true priest, the man who only lives for God and his fellow-men ...   Andrew Murray[49]

> To be sure this sacrifice of prayer, praise, and thanksgiving, and of ourselves as well, we are not to present before God in our own person. But we are to lay it upon Christ and let him present it for us ... We learn that we do not offer Christ as a sacrifice, but that Christ offers us.
>   Martin Luther[50]

Our Larger Task

Each Royal Priest holds office not merely for his or her own benefit. God's design is to touch others and all Creation with this renewed mind and subdued body.

> A priest is thus a man who does not live for himself. He lives with God and for God. His work as God's servant is to care for His house, His honor, and His worship, making known to men His love and His will. He lives with men and for men (Hebrews 5:2). His work is to find out their sins and needs, bring these before God, offer sacrifice and incense [prayers] in their names, obtain forgiveness and blessing for them, and then to come out and bless them in His Name.
>
> This is the high calling of every believer. They have been redeemed with the one purpose of being God's priests in the midst of the perishing millions around them. In conformity to Jesus, the Great High Priest, they are to be the ministers and stewards of the grace of God.
>
> Andrew Murray[51]

The Peace Offering [Shelem]

The name revolves around the Hebrew *shalom* and speaks not of a mere cessation of war or of a quietness of mind – actually it means "wholeness." When a jigsaw puzzle's contents are dumped out, although all the pieces are there, as long as the puzzle is not put together it is not "whole." When finally everything is as it should be and the picture can be fully seen, only then might you say that it has *shalom*.

There are many "pieces" in our lives: health; relationships with spouse, children, extended family, friends; activities and recreations; interests, attitudes, and perspectives; and many, many more. Central to this "picture," which is "the Image of God" in us, is our relationship with the Lord – that we, "beholding the Glory of the Lord as in a mirror, are being transformed into the same Image from glory to Glory, exactly as from the Lord the Spirit." [II Corinthians 3:18]. When all elements of a life are properly in their appropriate places, then we have *shalom;* but if some "pieces" are in the wrong places, some are missing, some are turned backward, some are in upside-down, and some simply do not belong, then there is no *shalom*.

Eastern meditation's "peace" calls on one to empty the mind, yet although it may bring a tranquility of sorts, it is not *shalom*. Its emptiness is like trying to erase the picture or to turn the puzzle to its reverse side – there is nothing there. This is not the Creator's design for His humans, as Jesus illustrates:

> When an unclean spirit goes out of a man, he goes through dry places, seeking rest, and finds none. Then he says, 'I will return to my house from which I came.' And when he comes, he finds it *empty, swept, and put in order*. Then he goes and takes with himself seven other spirits more wicked than himself, and they enter and dwell there; and the last state of that man is worse than the first... Matthew 12:43-45

This sacrifice calls not for an emptying of the mind but for a filling:

> For it is God Who said, 'Out of darkness light shall shine,' Who has shone in our hearts to illuminate the knowledge of the Glory of God in the face of Jesus Christ. II Corinthians 4:6

> ... through His Spirit in the inner man, that Christ may dwell through faith in your hearts; that you, being rooted and founded in Love, may have a full capacity to comprehend with all the saints what is the width, length, depth and height, and to know with transcending knowledge the Love of Christ; that you may be filled with all the fullness of God. Ephesians 3:16-21

The core of the New Testament *"Peace" Offering* is the special peace of Jesus: "Peace I leave with you, *My* peace I give to you; not as the world gives do I give to you" [John 14:27]:

> But now in Christ Jesus you, who once were far off, have become near in the Blood of Christ. For He Himself is our peace, having made both [Jew and Gentile] one, and has broken down the dividing wall of separation (the law of commands in the form of decrees/dogmas) – in His flesh He has ended the hostility. Now from the two He creates in Himself one new Man, thus making peace, and would reconcile both to God in one Body through the Cross, having put the hostility to death by means of it. Having come, He proclaimed the Gospel: peace to you who

were afar off and peace to those who were near, for through Him we both have the access by one Spirit to the Father. Ephesians 2:14-18

"For He Himself is our peace"; "create in Himself one new Man, thus making peace"; "would reconcile both to God in one Body through the Cross"; "through Him we both have the access by one Spirit to the Father" – it is not that Jesus *brings* peace, it is that Jesus *is* the Peace, "the Peace of God, which surpasses all understanding" [Philippians 4:7]. Just as the Old Testament *Peace Offering* was a type of communion, so also is this one. To have Peace, Jesus is both High Priest and Victim, giving to us His own Body and His own Blood in Holy Communion. It is only in this way that the *shalom* of the Old Testament *Peace Offering* can be truly fulfilled.

Entrusted with this sacrifice, the Royal Priests proclaim and encourage all who enter into God's Kingdom through Jesus' *Sin Offering* and through their willingness pictured in the *Whole Burnt Offering*, to participate in the powerful gift which Jesus holds before them in His *Peace Offering*.

The Thank Offering

P/ The Lord be with you!
C/ And also with you![52]

P/ Lift up your hearts!
C/ We lift them to the Lord!

P/ Let us give thanks to the Lord our God!
C/ It is right to give Him thanks and praise!

P/ It is truly good, right, and salutary that we should always and every-where thank You, holy Lord, almighty Father, everlasting God, [but chiefly are we bound to praise You for the glorious Resurrection of Your Son, Jesus Christ our Lord; He is the very Paschal Lamb offered for us, which has taken away the world's sins; Who by His death destroyed death and by His rising to life again restored to us everlasting life.]* Therefore, with angels and archangels and all the company of heaven we laud and magnify Your glorious Name, evermore praising You and singing:

C/ Holy, holy, holy Lord, God of pow'r and might: Heaven and earth are full of Your glory. Hosanna, Hosanna, Hosanna in the highest. Blessed is He Who comes in the Name of the Lord. Hosanna in the highest.
*(this changes to match the week's theme, here: Easter)

In this centuries-old part of the Liturgy, as it draws to the climax of the *Peace Offering* of Holy Communion, the *Thank Offerings* – thanksgiving – is to flow throughout the Royal Priests' activity. That is why this worship service is often called "the Eucharist," an ancient Greek word which combines "good" (*eu*) and "benefit, grace, gift" (*charis*) ("Good Gift/Good Grace" – Jesus' part), and as a single word means "thanksgiving, gratefulness" (the Church's response). Jesus set the context for this Sacrament when He blessed both the Bread and the Wine by giving thanks [Luke 22:17,19].

But as the Liturgy is the training ground for daily life, then

Whatever you do in word or deed, do all in the Name of the Lord Jesus, giving thanks to God the Father through Him.   Colossians 3:17

In everything give thanks; for this is the will of God in Christ Jesus for you.   I Thessalonians 5:18

The sacrifices in the New Testament context provide the basis for powerful hope and confidence as we face anything and everything in this world. We have the commitment of God Himself fully demonstrated in Jesus as both High Priest and designated Innocent Victim, and in the personal presence of the Holy Spirit. Although we may not always understand why, "It is truly good, right, and salutary that we should always and everywhere thank You, holy Lord, almighty Father, everlasting God."

Empowered Royal Priests

But now, for priestly consecration, there was to be closer contact with the blood. The ear, hand and foot were by a special act brought under its power, and the whole being sanctified for God. When the believer is led to seek full priestly access to God, he feels the need of a fuller and more enduring experience of the power of the blood. Where he had previously been content to have the blood sprinkled only on the mercy seat as what he needed for pardon, he now needs a more personal sprinkling, a cleansing of his heart from an evil conscience. Through this, he has "no more conscience of sin" (Hebrews 10:2); he is cleansed from all sin. As he gets to enjoy this, his consciousness is awakened to his wonderful right of intimate access to God, and the full assurance that his intercessions are acceptable.   Andrew Murray[53]

The Blood (the Life, the Soul) of the Sacrifice (Jesus) has intimate connection to the listening (ear), work (hand), and daily walk (toe) of the priests [Exodus 29:20] – which is a strong pointer to how Holy Communion is the continuing enabler for us to do our work of priesthood in this world. Unfortunately Murray does not take his description one verse farther; there the Blood is mixed with the anointing oil, which then is sprinkled upon the priests – the necessary companionship of the Holy Spirit in performing our tasks.

from Jesus Christ, the faithful Witness, the Firstborn from the dead, and the Ruler over the kings of the earth. To the One Who loves us, Who has washed us from our sins in His Blood, Who has made us kings and priests to His God and Father, to Him be Glory and dominion forever and ever. Amen.   Revelation 1:5-6

What is interesting is that the only other people who have this kind of consecration are the healed lepers [Leviticus 14]. Leprosy is a disease of insensitivity – it attacks the nerves, thereby making the person unable to notice the destruction the disease allows in his body. It is a powerful demonstration of the effect of sin. Might this be a declaration that the ones who have been most victim of sin can also, in the New Covenant, be among the most valuable of priests – that he who was deeply involved in sin, who has realized the extraordinary healing that Jesus' forgiveness has brought, is now one who is best equipped to priestly serve his fellow man?

When we can declare, with St John, "Yea, and our fellowship is with the Father and with His Son Jesus Christ" (I John I. 3), people will say the same of us: "They have been with Jesus!"   *The Kneeling Christian*[54]

8. Methods and Rituals *(See pages 31-34)*

Methods

The Sabbath Principle

> I tell you, something greater than the temple is here. If you had known what 'I desire mercy and not sacrifice' means, you would not have condemned the guiltless. For the Son of Man is Lord of the Sabbath.
>
> Matthew 12:6-8

> The Sabbath was made for man, not man for the Sabbath; so the Son of Man is Lord even of the Sabbath. Mark 2:27-28

Unfortunately there have been many arguments, even denominations divided, over what are really incidentals in regard to Baptism. How quickly we focus on mechanics rather than on the spirit of the relationship! But what really is Jehovah interested in? Jesus struggled against the same tendency of the Jews to focus on the insignificant in regard to the Sabbath and miss the real point of what really mattered. It is the same struggle in regard to the Sacraments:

> A Christian is holy in body and soul, whether he be layman or priest, man or woman. If anybody denies that, he speaks blasphemy against holy baptism, the blood of Christ, and the grace of the Holy Spirit. A Christian is a rare and wonderful thing, and God is more concerned about him than about the sacrament. For the Christian was not made for the sacrament, but the sacrament was instituted for the Christian.
>
> Martin Luther[55]

The most compelling aspect about Baptism is that the Creator wants this relationship with His treasured creatures. The method is merely and only the vehicle by which this is achieved. Although the mechanics can have importance, He ultimately is far more interested in the heart.

Yes, certain basics must be present: the Water, the Word and the Spirit [John 3:5; Ephesians 5:26; also Acts 8:35-38; 10:47-48]. Repentance and faith, which trusts God's work and Word, are necessary for the humble receiving of the benefits.

Anything else, be it method or additional ceremony, will not alter the effectiveness of this gift of grace. These things can be useful in identifying for the participant and observer the wondrous actions which the Creator is doing, teaching the people about the blessings of this relationship, as God is called upon to accomplish what He promised – but the additional ritual is not essential. Philip's Baptism of the Eunuch [Acts 8:36-39] likely was accompanied by very few formalities.

Many arguments on method are based upon the luxury of what is available, usually a lot of free flowing water. Yet Baptism must be available in all sorts of climates and conditions – what of the desert nomad or the Eskimo? What about the bedridden; the quadriplegic; the one with a tracheotomy or in an iron lung; the person about to face surgery? What about the person in a hostile setting, such as under a Muslim regime, where Baptisms must be done in secret? Can we bind God's act of grace only to a method based on what is convenient here?

For something that our Lord has powerfully wanted to do, it is dangerous for us to forbid Him the ability to act until *we* are satisfied that the method and conditions meet *our* standards. Throughout the book of Acts, the instruction is that the Baptism be done immediately, not until such time as the circumstances are appropriate. The idea of waiting conveys that Baptism is merely a nice "romantic," even incidental, thing to do, rather than having the essential urgency of Jesus' words to Nicodemus, "Very truly I tell you, unless one is born of the Water and the Spirit, he is not able to enter God's Kingdom" [John 3:5].

Different Methods

In considering the method of Baptism, it is crucial to realize that there is no passage that says "this is how you do it." Rather the "how" is only something that we infer from different passages and words, and as such cannot be binding, since such deductions depend more on the person than on the passage.

On one hand, "Baptize" (*Baptidzo*) and "Baptism" (*baptismos*) are the most common references to this act of grace. This word covers the range from submerging into water, to bathing (which does not necessarily mean full immersion), washing and cleaning (which does not necessarily require the item to be standing in much water.). Some passages using this word are Mark 7:4; Luke 11:38; Acts 1:5, 11:16; Acts 22:16; Romans 6:4; I Corinthians 12:13; Galatians 3:27; and Hebrews 9:10.

"Wash" (*Louo*) and "bath" (*loutron*) are also a frequent word group which covers such ideas as to bathe or wash a dead person, or to wash Blood out of wounds. Passages where this can be found are Acts 22:16; I Corinthians 6:11; Ephesians 5:25-26; Titus 3:5; Hebrews 10:22, II Peter 2:22; and Revelation 7:14.

There is also the concept of "pouring out," for example, of the Spirit in Acts 2:17-18, 33 [Joel 2:28-29]; other passages would be Ezekiel 39:29; Zechariah 12:10; and Romans 5:5. And "sprinkling" must also be included:

> let us approach with a true heart in full confidence of faith, the hearts being sprinkled from an evil conscience and the bodies washed with pure water. …
> For if the Blood of bulls and goats, and the ashes of a heifer [Red heifer, a cleansing from death] sprinkled on those who have been defiled sanctifies as to the purging of the flesh, how much more will the Blood of Christ Who, through the eternal Spirit offered Himself without blemish to God, will purge your conscience from dead works to rather serve the living God. …

For when Moses had spoken every precept to all the people according to the Law, he took the Blood of calves and goats, with water, scarlet wool, and hyssop, and sprinkled both the book itself and all the people, saying, "This is the Blood of the Covenant which God has commanded you."

Likewise the Tent of Meeting and all the vessels of the "liturgy"/ministry he sprinkled with Blood – indeed, almost all things are purged/cleansed with Blood according to the Law, and apart from the shedding of Blood there is no forgiveness.

Hebrews 10:22; 9:13-14, 19-20, 21-22

I will sprinkle clean water upon you, and you shall be clean from all your defilement; I will cleanse you from all your idols; I will give you a new heart; I will put within you a new spirit; I will take the heart of stone out of your flesh and I will give you a heart of flesh; I will put My Spirit within you, and I will make My statutes for you to walk in, and My judgments for you to keep and do.

Ezekiel 36:25-27

Immersion

"Immersion" is inferred by St Paul's concept of "buried with Him in baptism" [Colossians 2:12], and the picture is effective, that of going down and drowning, dying, but then rising up to new life. But however useful this image is, it was not the Jewish concept of Baptism prior to Jesus:

The meanings of "to drown," "to sink" or "to perish" seem to be quite absent from the Heb. and Aram. [*HBL*] and therefore from [*baptidzein*] in Jewish Greek.   *TDNT*[56]

In other words, when John the Baptist baptized Jesus, there is nothing in the Old Testament theology which would have this concept; and even the disciples' baptism done during Jesus' ministry [John 3:22; 4:2] would not have such a Resurrection interpretation, since they did not yet even understand about their Lord's death.

There are archaeological and logistic problems: three thousand were Baptized on Pentecost in Jerusalem, where no river nor other large quantities of water exists. Poor water supplies in general in many parts of the ancient world would make immersion unlikely.

> It is unlikely that in Jerusalem, Samaria, Damascus, Philippi, Corinth, Rome, or Asia Minor enough water was always available for a full bath.
> *The Interpreter's Dictionary of the Bible*[57]

The earliest Christian artwork (tile mosaics in ancient churches and paintings in the catacombs) often show the recipient standing in the river while water is poured over his head from a cup or shell; and an early Christian baptistery in a church in Nazareth, circa second century, was too small and narrow in which to immerse a person.

The *Didache* ["Teachings"/"Doctrine"], circa 70 AD (40 years after the crucifixion), instructs:

> Concerning baptism, baptize in this manner: Having said all these things beforehand, baptize in the name of the Father and of the Son and of the Holy Spirit in living water [running water]. If there is no living water, baptize in other water; and, if you are not able to use cold water, use warm. If you have neither, pour water three times upon the head in the name of the Father, Son, and Holy Spirit.   Didache 7:1-3[58]

Although the imagery of full immersion is useful, so also is the concept of "washing," while "pouring" and "sprinkling" also have valid Old Testament symbolisms. The best conclusion is that there is no proscribed method of Baptism: *any* way of applying the Water and the Word is valid and will be honored by our Lord's promises. Still, the method can be used as a way of teaching something about what happens in this Sacrament – in fact, one might consider rotating through all the methods, of course depending on conditions and circumstances, as a teaching tool on the variety of blessings within this Sacrament.

Rituals

The Sign of the Cross

Perhaps we have seen a TV show or film in which someone makes "the Sign of the Cross" during a crisis or upon a death. Sadly, it is likely that most people have no idea what this means. First of all, "sign" is a Covenant word:

The Scar
Since Covenant is "cut," it has an essential spin-off: a 'SIGN.' As two humans cut Covenant, most often the SIGN is a scar – a continuing, indelible, and often public – reminder and guarantee of Covenant.

A woman with native-American background once described how her grandfather had three 'Blood-brothers,' and the wound from cutting the palm was picked at in order to make the scar prominent – an obvious and proud reminder of his Covenant-relationships. Such a SIGN is also a constant reminder of one's grave responsibility, and at the same time, of comfort – it is a message to any enemy that a Blood-brother has pledged to defend – and avenge – his Covenant-partner.

James Lindemann[59]

Pastor: Receive the Sign of the Holy Cross, both upon the forehead [✝] and upon the heart [✝], in token that you have been redeemed by Christ the Crucified. From an adaption of Luther's Taufburchlein [1526]

In Circumcision, Blood flows and Covenant-Blood "mingles," and results in an unmistakable *"sign"* impossible to remove, evidence that *"My Covenant in your flesh* is an everlasting Covenant" [Genesis 17:13].

Although not a *physical* "sign" like Circumcision, this New Covenant counterpart of "the Sign of the Cross" is just as indelible. It is Jehovah's mark before the universe, angel and devil alike, that this person is *His.* When Moses is sent to Egypt to bring God's People out from slavery, he is given three "signs" [Exodus 4:1-9]: the staff that becomes a serpent, the leprous hand, and the water turned to Blood. The *first* people to whom Moses shows these "signs" are the Israelites [vv 29-31], and only subsequently does he show them to Pharaoh [5:8-17] – why? Because the same "signs" are for comfort to those in Covenant, reminding them that they do not stand alone, whereas to an enemy, the "sign" is a warning that when one trifles with this People, they trifle with the Covenant-Partner, the Lord God Almighty Himself.

So for the Christian, "the Sign of the Cross" is the reminder not just of who he is, but especially of *Whose* he is. The "sign" is God's "royal mark" – His seal, proof, and reminder of the extraordinary relationship through Jesus into which Baptism sets us. It is also the warning to any foe (human, satanic, death, nature or whatever) that as weak as the Christian may seem, there is the Almighty One Who stands with him. It is interesting that in the Dracula fictional lore, "the Sign of the Cross" would terrify the Count. One wonders if anyone from writer to actors ever understood why.

It is an indelible, eternal "sign," because the relationship we are set into is such. It is no automatic ticket to heaven, but just like the relationship of the prodigal son to his father [Luke 15:11-24], it remains always ready to be revitalized:

> [Regarding Augustine's view:] Although the nonbeliever does not receive grace, he does not remain untouched by Baptism and is not the same after Baptism as he was before. For through Baptism the "distinguishing mark of the Lord" has been stamped upon him similar to the "royal mark" that was given soldiers, or the impress of a coin or seal. The nonbeliever, too, has been made Christ's property.
>
> If he later comes to faith, he is not re-baptized, but assured of forgiveness by the laying on of hands and now the grace becomes effective ...
>
> [Luther held likewise views,] but he was less concerned about what happened to the nonbeliever in Baptism than about what God has placed at the nonbeliever's disposal through Baptism ... therefore the reference to the Baptism of the nonbeliever as "a treasure."
>
> Edmund Schlink[60]

The Chrisom

In some rituals a Chrisom or Baptismal cloth is spread over the Baptized, and the Pastor says something like the following:

> As you are now clothed with this pure, white, unspotted garment, so may you evermore be clothed with the righteousness and innocence of our dear Lord and Savior Jesus Christ, for Whose sake God has made you His child and received you as an heir of eternal life. "For as many of you as have been Baptized into Christ have put on Christ" [Galatians 3:27].   From an adaption of Luther's Taufburchlein [1526]

In Jesus' parable of the wedding feast [Matthew 22:2-14], a guest was challenged for not wearing a wedding garment. It was usually a long white robe provided to each guest by the host of the feast. Having rejected this garment, this man would be in his common ordinary dress, for he was taken from the highway. Even if he were in the finery of a noble, without the robe for which the king was looking, he had no excuse as it demonstrated the highest disrespect for this host.

In Isaiah 1:18, Jehovah says, "Come now, and let us reason together, … though your sins are like scarlet, they shall be as white as snow; though they are red like crimson, they shall be as wool." Scarlet and crimson stand out unmistakably. Even in our limited spiritual field of vision, there are sins and foolishnesses which stick out as equally vivid whenever we look over our lives. If we were to face the Host of the Wedding Feast of the Last Day just on this basis alone, we also would be embarrassed, much more if we consider Isaiah 64:6, "… all our righteousnesses are like filthy rags."

But in Ephesians 5:25-27, St Paul describes how Jesus has cleansed His People "by the washing of Water in the Word, that He might present her to Himself, the Glorious Church, not having spot or defect or any such thing, but that she should be holy and without blemish." This is the "white robe" of Revelation 6:11 and 7:13-14 washed in the Blood of the Lamb. And just

150

as scarlet and crimson under a red light become white, under the light of the forgiveness of the Blood of Jesus our sins become white as snow. Snow is an intriguing image because it softens a harsh landscape, rounds sharp edges and even makes the town dump into a beautiful place.

This, of course, is the righteousness of Jesus which is given by grace, which clothes us when we have "put on Christ" as symbolized by the Chrisom.

The Light

> Receive this lighted candle in token that you have received Christ Jesus, the Light of the world -- "So let your Light shine, that all may see your good works, and glorify your Father Who is in heaven." [Matthew 5:16].
> From an adaption of Luther's Taufburchlein [1526]

Another tradition has been to give to the Baptized, particularly children a lighted candle. As with many rituals, it also simply describes what has already occurred within this Sacrament: the Light of the World has entered our lives and we are called upon to let the world see Him in us.

In a sense, the candle is an educational tool. It is meant to be burned on each Baptismal birthday. What child (or even adult) does not like the idea of having two birthday parties a year (especially if there is cake!)? It is suggested that if the Godparents desire to give gifts to the child either for his birthday or Christmas, it should rather be at this time, thereby accenting that something very special occurred on this day.

The intent is to make the child curious about why there is this celebration, especially when many of her friends do not have such an occasion. This becomes what educators call "the teachable moment" – what is shared now with the child will "stick" in his memory. Therefore a devotion or a reading accenting some aspect of Baptism would be helpful.

The Sign of the Anointing

Using anointing oil, in some rituals the Pastor marks a Cross on the forehead of the Baptized, saying:

> **P/** Receive this anointing in token that you have received the grace of God, the gift of the Holy Ghost; that you might ever continue steadfast in the grace and knowledge of our Lord Jesus Christ, and be empowered to carry out your lifelong responsibility of being prophet, priest and royal child in God's Kingdom.
>
> From an adaption of Luther's Taufburchlein [1526]

> At our Baptism God also gives us a gift beyond every measure – the gift of the Holy Spirit. By the sign of anointing, the applying of oil, this gift is signified. Throughout Scripture ..., prophets, priests and kings were anointed signifying that the Holy Spirit had come upon them. It was a momentous thing in the Old Testament when the Holy Spirit came upon those who were anointed, but in the New Testament we have a different, new and wonderful relationship. St Paul says: "What! Know you not that you are a temple of the Holy Ghost, which is in you and which you have of God?" [I Corinthians 6:19] All the way through the New Testament this close relationship is emphasized. They were God's People, we are His children. There God's presence was signified by the Shekinah, the cloud, going with them or resting upon the tabernacle. But we know "the mystery which hath been hid from the ages, which is Christ in you, the Hope of glory" [Colossians 1:27].
>
> Robert Lindemann[61]

Just as much as "the Sign of the Cross" is an important spiritual confirmation of our relationship to the Jehovah of Covenant, so also the anointing of the Holy Spirit not only equips us for our life as God's People and Christ's Body, He is the constant reminder that our relationship is not static but is alive and acting.

> But you are not in the flesh but in the Spirit, if indeed the Spirit of God dwells in you. If anyone does not have the Spirit of Christ, he is not His. But if Christ *is* in you, although the body is dead because of sin, the Spirit has life through righteousness. ...
>
> For you did not receive a spirit of slavery to again be afraid, but you have received the Spirit of sonship, in whom we cry, "Abba! Father!" –

the Spirit Himself bears witness with our spirit that we are God's children.   Romans 8:9-10, 15-16

This is how we are empowered to be the "prophets" (those who speak the Word and will of God) who "proclaim the praises of Him Who called you out of darkness into His marvelous light" [I Peter 2:9], the "royal priesthood" who bring the praises and needs of Creation to Jehovah and His blessings and forgiveness to creation, and the "kings" who represent the Glory of "the King" in all of life.

Being "Earnest"

In II Corinthians 1:22 (also 5:5) we are not only sealed (marked, as by the Cross, as our Lord's possession), but as the King James Version put it, God has "given *the earnest* of the Spirit in our hearts":

> In Whom ye also trusted, after that ye heard the Word of Truth, the Gospel of your salvation: in Whom also after that ye believed, ye were sealed with that Holy Spirit of promise, Which is *the earnest* of our inheritance until the redemption of the purchased possession, unto the praise of His glory.   Ephesians 1:13-14 (KJV)

There is a reason why the King James Version chose the word "earnest" instead of "guarantee." In the seventeenth century, rarely was a "down-payment" ever made; but when it did happen, it was because the purchaser was showing that he was "in earnest" about completing the transaction – hence its name "earnest." Not only does Jehovah declare to the universe that we are His, the Holy Spirit is God demonstrating *to us* how much "in earnest" *He* is (rather than requiring earnestness on our part). So powerful is this commitment that St Paul can say, "confident of this very thing, that He Who began a good work in you will bring it to completion at the day of Jesus Christ" [Philippians 1:6].

Because God is the only source of real life, and His holiness excludes sin... The significance of baptism thus depends on the fact that it is a real action of the holy God in relation to sinful man. Hence both a superstitious and also purely symbolical understanding are excluded.

...Though mediated by men, baptism is the action of God or Christ (Eph 5:26). *TDNT*[62]

9. Living Water[63] (See pages 35-38)

Old Testament Depth

A Peculiar Phrase

"Living Water" is a most curious phrase – but perhaps to dryland or desert people, running water might have been considered as living and life-giving. Indeed that may be the usage in Genesis 26:19's "a well of 'living' waters," and also in Song of Solomon 4:15. These are the only two apparently secular uses of the term in the Bible.

However, in the sacrifices for the cleansing from leprosy (a living death) [Leviticus 14], "the Living Waters" is paired with "the living bird" (as opposed to the second bird, "the killed bird"); this suggests that the concept goes far deeper than merely "running water." In fact, in Deuteronomy 21:3-9, there is a different word used for "running water," so that it is not as if the Hebrew language has no alternate descriptions.

The term really shifts into dramatic gear in Jeremiah and Zechariah. Jehovah describes Himself as "the Fountain of Living Waters" [Jeremiah 2:13; 17:13] and in Zechariah [14:8] the end time is characterized by "Living Waters shall go out from Jerusalem."

It would reach its climax during the prophesied time of the New Covenant (the image of "water" is used here, even though the term "Living Water" is not used): "For I will pour Waters on the thirsty, and Streams on the land; I will pour My Spirit on your seed (descendants), and My blessing on your offspring" [Isaiah 44:3].

The Red Heifer and "Living Water" – *Numbers 19*

Much uncleanness in the Old Covenant is purified by a bath, a change of clothes and the change of day. However, like a deadly poison or contagious disease, death is so invasively contaminating that mere contact with it renders a person unclean for a whole week. *Any* contact with death or those among the 'living dead' (lepers) demands a restoration to Life. The Red Heifer's Sacrifice is given for such a purpose.

Among this Sacrifice's unique features are: the *red* [that is, Blood/Life] heifer is killed *outside* the camp (v 3; not at the door of *the Tent of Meeting* or by *the Altar of Sacrifice*, as is *every other sacrifice AND slaughtered animal* – as Jesus also suffers *"outside the gate"* [Hebrews 13:12-13]) and is burned *with* her Blood (v 5; it is *not* poured out before the altar as every other *Sin Offering*'s Blood is) along with cedar (*red*-wood), *scarlet* wool and hyssop (a combination mentioned elsewhere only for the cleansing of the leper [Numbers 14]).

The gathered-up ashes are added to *"Living Waters"* [Numbers 19:17] (which now become "the Waters of Impurity" [v 9]) to be sprinkled, only by another who is already clean, on those whom death has touched – who after seven days now become restored to the Life of God's People (they are allowed to enter the camp) and are therefore also restored in their Covenant relationship with God (since *the Tent of Meeting* was in the center of the camp).

Despite death having such power, this Sacrifice's potency is so great that apparently only six heifers have been needed throughout all the generations between Moses and the destruction of the Temple in 70 AD[64] (Jesus would be *the seventh and final sacrifice!*[65]) – it is as close to an eternal sacrifice as one can get. But woe to him who does not "need" it: "that Soul will be cut off from among the assembly, for he has defiled *the Sanctuary* of Jehovah" [v 20].

"Living Waters" mixed with the Sacrifice of the Red Heifer's ashes provide the antidote for death and therefore for the reconnection to the Source of Life and to His People – what a powerful image of what Jesus will be and do!

New Testament "Living Water"

Turning On the Fountain

Jesus answered her, "If you knew the Gift of God, and Who He is Who is saying to you, 'Give Me a drink,' you would have asked Him, and He would have given you Living Water …

"Every one drinking of this water will thirst again, but whoever drinks from the Water which I shall give him, in no way will he thirst in this world age; but the Water that I will give him will become in him a spring of Water springing up into Eternal Life." John 4:7,13-14

"He who believes in Me, as the Scripture has said, 'from the center of his being will flow Living Water.'" But He said this about the Spirit, Whom those believing in Him were about to receive, for the Holy Spirit was not yet sent, because Jesus was not yet glorified. John 7:38-39

"The Water and the Blood" flow from Jesus' side and in I John 5:8 these are connected to "the Spirit" as *witnesses*, the same "Spirit" which John 7 associates with "the Living Water." Then to Nicodemus [John 3:5], Jesus speaks of how "born of the Water and the Spirit" is absolutely essential to "enter the Kingdom of God." Here then in Baptism is the Fountain of Life which accomplishes between Jehovah and the individual the new relationship as described throughout this book.

As a side note, in the Hebrew language there is noun form which is between "singular" and "plural" – it is called "dual," which specifically indicates only two of the item:

Special Dual Nouns. There are three special Hebrew words that are *always dual in form* but normally singular in translation: ... (heaven, heavens), ... (Egypt), and ... (water). *Basics of Biblical Hebrew*[66]

This "dual" actually fits in our discussion because the Fountain is two-fold, two "waters" in Baptism, the one from the side of Jesus, the cleansing flood, but there is also the Holy Spirit, described as a Fountain of "Living Water."

The Gift of the Holy Spirit

Peter said to them, "Repent, and be Baptized every one of you in the Name of Jesus Christ into the forgiveness of your sins; and you will receive the gift of the Holy Spirit." Acts 2:38

In the John 7 quote above, the Holy Spirit is directly tied in with the "rivers of Living Water," and Peter here states that the main result of Baptism is the active presence of God the Holy Spirit in the life of the Baptized. It is important to note that Peter does not say "you *need to* receive the gift" as if it is a two-stage process where one must make the conditions right to achieve the second stage, but rather this *gift* comes as an immediate promise, as the consequence of Baptism.

Acts 2:38 doesn't stop with forgiveness, though. It goes on. ... When Peter addresses the amazed onlookers, he explains that that day was the fulfillment of Joel's prophecy [2:28-32] that the Spirit would be poured out. There's another very similar prophecy that I think sheds light on Acts 2. Ezekiel 36:24-27 prophesies a future day when the Lord would sprinkle water upon His people and cleanse them from their impurities, their sin, and put a new Spirit in them. As in Ezekiel, the forgiveness of sins and the gift of the Spirit are connected and related to water, in this case water baptism. And did you notice how the Spirit is simply promised to all who are baptized. There are no conditions attached. It's simply a promise of God. There is no second or subsequent stage in the Christian life. Christians are all to be granted the Holy Spirit. There's no such thing as a "have-not" Christian. Andrew Das[67]

158

The only times when the Holy Spirit's bestowal is very conspicuous are the watershed events in the expansion of the Gospel – there is the sense that the highlighted bestowal, rather than normative, instead indicates divine confirmation as a sort of "firstfruits" as each of Jesus' target "fields" are opened:

> You shall receive power when the Holy Spirit has come upon you; and you shall be witnesses of Me both in Jerusalem, and in all Judea and Samaria, and to the end of the earth.   Acts 1:8

The only times in which the Holy Spirit's bestowal is highlighted are:

1. When the Church as God's New Nation is established [Acts 2], the evangelistic field which begins at Jerusalem, but then naturally extends into Judea.

2. When Philip "converts" the Samaritans (*not* Gentiles but rather those of "the household of Israel" who had deliberately deviated from the faith) [Acts 8:5-17]. Here the apostles are needed to bestow the Spirit;
   yet when Philip "converts" the Ethiopian Eunuch [v 39], there is no stated additional bestowal, even though the Eunuch would initiate a mission field of his own;
   nor is a separate stage mentioned after St Paul's Baptism [9:17-18].

3. When the door to the Gentiles (all nations) is "officially" opened [10:44-48]; recounted in 11:15-18.

4. When "Disciples" in Ephesus with only John's Baptism [19:1-6] are reBaptized. They now receive that fullness which John had predicted.

The Witness

When Jesus declares "you shall be My witnesses," Acts 5:32 agrees: "We are His witnesses to these things ('words'), and so also is the Holy Spirit Whom God has given to those who obey Him," and there are echoes here of John's three witnesses [I John 5:6 8 – see chapter 2], "the Spirit, the Water, and the Blood." As witnesses, their business is to declare the essential message – the Good News – of the reality of Jesus' salvation and of the new and powerful connection we can have with the Creator of the universe forever.

The Holy Spirit, bestowed once-for-all-time in our Baptism, is our ongoing equipment for this new lifetime of relationships. He is not merely an option or an add-on – He is much too pivotal a key player in all that occurs in Baptism, equipping *all* within the Body of Christ for daily life as God's People. After all, He is essential: to "understand the gifts bestowed on us by God" [I Corinthians 2:12]; to confess "Jesus is Lord" [I Corinthians 12:3]; to pour into our hearts "God's love" [Romans 5:5]; to help "us in our weakness" [Romans 8:26]; to bring together those "who were far off and ... those who were near" so that "we both have access in one Spirit to the Father" demonstrating that we "are fellow citizens with the saints and of the household of God" [Ephesians 2:19; I Corinthians 12:13]; to be "changed into the same Image from one degree of Glory to another" [II Corinthians 3:18]; to make "the offering of the Gentiles ... acceptable, sanctified by the Holy Spirit" [Romans 15:16].

> there are diversities of gifts, but the same Spirit;
> there are diversities of service, but the same Lord;
> there are diversities of working, but it is the same God Who works all things in all.
>   To each is given the manifestation of the Spirit for the common good: ... wisdom ... knowledge ... faith ... healing ... miracles ... prophecy ... ability to distinguish between spirits ... tongues ... interpretation of tongues. All these are inspired by one and the same Spirit, Who apportions to each one individually as He wills.
>   II Corinthians 12:4-11

Paul asserts that the Holy Spirit has gifted each person in some way – each has a valuable contribution to make and what the Spirit gives each will not necessarily be predictable – it is "as He wills":

The wind blows where it wills – you hear its sound but you do not know from where it comes and to where it goes. So is everyone who is born of the Spirit. John 3:8

However, just as the Glory of God are attributes only visible in action, so also are the basic signs of the Spirit's work in Jesus' Church:

Acts provides ample evidence that the people DO receive the gift of the Spirit. Luke does not narrate a mass phenomenon of 3,000 people speaking in tongues. Rather, what Luke describes is a Spirit-filled community that came together for the breaking of bread, the apostles' teaching, fellowship and prayer. The early believers held all things in common. Actually, all throughout Luke's Gospel and Acts, how you use your possessions is a sign of your inner condition and status before God. Andrew Das[68]

And so also is the fruit of the Spirit: "Love, joy, peace, longsuffering, kindness, goodness, faithfulness, gentleness, self–control" [Galatians 5:22-23] a reflection of God's Glory *in action* as Christians live out being "the Image" and "the [Soul-] Likeness" of the Creator.

Filled

The fountain has now been opened, we are bid to plunge our cup into the "Living Waters" and drink deeply of the Holy Spirit:

Do not get drunk with wine, which is wastefulness; but be filled with the Spirit, speaking to each other in psalms and hymns and spiritual songs, singing and making melody in your heart to the Lord, at all times and for all things giving thanks in the Name of our Lord, Jesus Christ, to God the Father. Ephesians 5:18-20

Reading the Word, group Bible study, worship, singing, music, prayer, giving thanks, Holy Communion, helping each other – these are some of the many ways by which we can become "filled," not as a one-time experience but frequently as we go about living within our Lord's Covenant. The Holy Spirit will fill us also to make us suitable for a short- or even a long-term task

161

which He has chosen for us, as He did the unborn John the Baptist [Luke 1:15,41] or when his father Zechariah was empowered to prophesy or when Steven faced his final persecution [Acts 7:55] – such an "equipping" occurs within the context of the Body of Christ being who they are:

> When they had prayed, the place in which they were assembled was shaken; and they all were filled with the Holy Spirit and spoke the Word of God with boldness.   Acts 4:31

> The disciples were filled with joy and with the Holy Spirit [despite just being persecuted!]   Acts 13:9

Once Opened

Opening the faucet on the Fountain needs be done only once.

A subsequent Baptism would be like a remarriage ceremony on the 40th anniversary – nothing is really changed legally, physically or relationship-wise, however it may have positive effects on the couple's relationship.

The Old Testament has many subsequent Covenants, and a useful reference point in this regard would be Jonathan and David. They cut their first Covenant in I Samuel 18:1, 3 and in reality nothing can change the total commitment each has to the other. After all, if the Life/Blood from the first Covenant still flows in the veins, and the core of one's being (Soul) is joined to the core of the other's being (Soul), then what more could any subsequent Covenant provide?

However, in their second Covenant [I Samuel 20:14-17], 'reopening the wound' reopens the Covenant to a specific oath to *reassure Jonathan*. Since the whole family is already implicitly included in the first, nothing new is really added, yet it brings comfort as it confirms that his posterity is understood as included. Their *third* Covenant [I Samuel 23:16-18] is *to reassure David*: during David's flight from Saul, Jonathan comes to "strengthen his hand in God." Again, since the original commitment is still irrevocably in effect, it also adds nothing new, but simply comforts David in that his Covenant-partner does indeed stand firmly by him.

Once Baptism's floodgate is open, it is open. Nothing can be changed by a subsequent ceremony. On the other hand, there seems to be nothing Scriptural to forbid, for example, a person visiting the Holy Land from being Baptized in the River Jordan as a sense of participating in the great events that have occurred there. Likely Jonathan and David would understand.

There is a real danger though and therefore subsequent Baptisms should be discouraged. Very easily our human nature can latch on to this as if it were a special mark of piety ("See, I've been Baptized *five* times!"), and besides, Circumcision obviously could only be done once. Actually there is a better solution than subsequent Baptisms, which is Holy Communion. Subsequent Baptisms degenerate into mere rituals, whereas if Communion is understood rightly, it is a "right-now" *action and presence* of Jesus as He allows us to mutually participate in everything He is and has, and He with us.

Never-ending "Living Water"

> He brought me to the door of the House; and behold, water was flowing from under the threshold of the House toward the east ... He led me by way of the north gate, outside to the outer gateway that faces east; and water was boiling out on the right side.
> The man went to the east with the line in his hand and measured one thousand cubits; he passed me through the waters and the water came to the ankles. He measured another thousand; he led me through the waters and the water came to the knees. He measured yet another thousand; when he brought me through, the water came to the waist. Again he measured one thousand, and it was a torrent which I could not cross – the water had so risen that it was a water which one must swim, a river through which could not be walked ... along the bank of the river, were very many trees on one side and the other. ...

It shall be that every soul that lives, wherever the rivers go, will live. …
Along the bank of the river, on this side and that, will grow all kinds of
trees used for food; its leaf will not fade, and its fruit will not fail. It will
bear fruit every month, because its water flows from the sanctuary. Its
fruit will be for food, and its leaf for healing.   Ezekiel 47:1-12

He showed me a pure river of the Water of Life, clear as crystal, coming
out from the throne of God and of the Lamb. In the midst of its street,
and on both sides of the river, was the Tree of Life producing twelve
fruits, yielding each one according to the month. The leaves of the Tree
were for the healing of the nations.   Revelation 22:1-2

This is impressive! The little flow of water from the Temple rapidly
increases to overwhelming proportions, but as Revelation takes up the
picture, it is part of the description of Jesus' rule into eternity.

It should be noted again, that in a bit of a twist, our version of "heaven"
is when we get to be with God – but Jehovah's version is when *He* gets to be
with *us*: "Behold, the dwelling of God is with men. He will dwell with them,
they will be His People, and God Himself will be their God with them"
[Revelation 21:3; also Ezekiel 37:26-27]. Actually this only a continuation of
what the Holy Spirit has started by making His home in us [I Corinthians
3:16-17; 6:19] and of Jesus' promise, "We will come to him and make Our
home with him" [John 14:23].

The evidence is that the "flow" of the Holy Spirit, the "flood" of the
blessings, His sharing of "the Living Waters" of our Baptism will never
cease – even when sin is no longer part of the picture, the relationship that
Baptism has given us just will never end!

So, Does Baptism Really Save Us?

No Automatic Entry-Pass

From this fact, however, the Scriptures do not permit us to conclude
that Baptism through its mere performance, whether at infancy or any

other stage of a person's life, automatically or mechanically insures deliverance from final judgment. Rather, because it places not just a moment or an hour but the whole of a man's life from birth to death under the promise and sign of the cross, Baptism is the ceaseless urging of God's grace seeking to become continually and repeatedly effective in the person's actual daily existence. As the action of grace, not of irresistible force, Baptism's gift and blessing can be rejected and lost. The power to reject it lies with man. The power to respond to Baptism's "holy calling" comes with the gracious call itself. ...

... Only when Baptism itself, including the Baptism of infants, informs our whole Christian vision, only when it is seen in terms of its far-reaching, continually practical and daily implications for ordering and shaping the entire Christian existence and life – of both church and individual – only then does it really come into its own as the means of God's grace.   Richard Jungkuntz[69]

"The whole of a man's life from birth to death" – the action may not be repeated, but now once the flowing "Water of Life" has been started, it is not to be turned off. The Fountain refers to the presence of the Holy Spirit, and now He has been "released" into our lives – now He will be at work to bring more and more blessing into our lives in a greater and greater flood. More and more He will show us what it is to be the Children of God, the Body of Christ, and fellow citizens of the Kingdom of God.

Yet there is also a note of warning:

For those who once were enlightened, who tasted the heavenly Gift, who became partakers in the Holy Spirit, who tasted the goodness of God's Word, of the power and of the age to come, and who then fall away, it is impossible to restore them to repentance, since they crucify again for themselves the Son of God and hold Him up to contempt.
                                                             Hebrews 6:4-6

This is not a game to play at, but rather to understand that we can "grieve the Holy Spirit of God" [Ephesians 4:30], and even "quench the Spirit" [I Thessalonians 5:19]. How we treat the extraordinary gift of the Fountain of the Water of Life is important. Still it is equally important to remember that whenever we seriously repent, like the Prodigal Son we will receive not only a welcome but also a celebration.

Yet a Definite Connection is Made

> [The salvation through Noah's Ark] was a prototype of Baptism, which now saves you, not as a putting away of the filth of the flesh but the answer of a clear conscience to God, through the resurrection of Jesus Christ   I Peter 3:21

Peter's answer is yes, "Baptism ... now saves you." But not as merely a ritual. But not as an item which stands by itself. It is because Baptism is linked with repentance, faith, the "flood" of the Holy Spirit and the work of Jesus as it flows from His side – therefore yes, it does save us. We now have a Covenant connection with God which surpasses Circumcision in the Old Testament. Herein lies the opportunity to directly experience Jehovah Himself *in us*, because this is His desire and He commands it.

But what of the thief on the cross who probably never experienced this Sacrament? Obviously the relationship with God is not denied him: "today you will be with Me in paradise" [Luke 23:43]. Clearly Jehovah is not limited by His directive to us – we are bound to Baptize whenever possible, we have no choice, we are under command, but *He* is not limited in this way. When we cannot and do not have opportunity to carry out His instruction, we can still entrust the unbaptized into the hands of Him "Who is able to do exceedingly abundantly above all that we ask or think" [Ephesians 3:20]. We cannot make decisions for our Lord, but we also have seen the Cross and His Steadfast Love and so are confident that He will apply His mercy and grace as His heart and His justice will allow.

Jesus' Baptism

Part of how Baptism saves us is also found in Jesus' Baptism. But we are confused – "Arise and be Baptized, and wash away your sins, calling on the Name of the Lord" [Acts 22:16] – however Jesus has no sin, so why is He Baptized?

Since Baptism involves repentance, imagine how the Baptismal waters have become loaded with sins. Like in the pioneer days when bath night starts with the youngest, then more hot water is added with each next older's bath, one wonders if the last person becomes cleaner or dirtier by taking the bath. So also with Jesus as He steps into the sin-clogged Baptismal waters. He cannot become cleaner, rather all the sins stick to Him. This moment of His Baptism begins His ministry as the Sin-Bearer, taking all our sins upon Himself. As St Paul puts it, "For God made Him to be sin for us, Who knew no sin" [II Corinthians 5:21]. This touches on Ephesians 5:26, where *Jesus* is described as washing us with the Water and the Word – although washed off of us, He has taken them upon Himself. And so, we are made clean. This is indeed a saving act – Baptism does save us.

There is a comforting side benefit to Jesus' Baptism. Much too often in our sin we are in "hot water," yet in Baptism, we look over and find Jesus has placed Himself beside us in the same water. As soon as He steps into this water, He becomes a sinner – *just like us* – not that He *does* any sin, but rather because He carries our sins. He is condemned to death – *just like we deserve* – because of the sin that He carries. Yet for *us* the water becomes cooler – becomes a *bath* water – as Paul continues, "so that, *in him*, we are made the righteousness of God." He has indeed come "to *fulfill* all righteousness" as He tells John the Baptist [Matthew 3:13-15] – He comes to fulfill *ours*.

Everywhere in our spiritual life we will find Jesus right along with us. In death, we look over and find that He "stands in the water with us." In the Resurrection, we see that the King is one *of* us – and one *with* us.

So, in His Baptism, He does not come to walk *on* the water, but to step *in* the water – not daintily sticking His toe in, but plunging into our lives, our worlds, our hearts, even our sin-tainted bodies. Yes, He is in this as deeply as we are, because He is in us.

Baptism's Ultimate Conclusion

> He said to me, "It is done! I am the Alpha and the Omega, the Beginning and the End. I will give of the fountain of the Water of Life freely to him who thirsts." ...
> The Spirit and the Bride say, "Come!" And let him who hears say, "Come!" And let him who thirsts come. Whoever desires, let him take the Water of Life freely. Revelation 21:6; 22:17

What God worked toward throughout the Old Covenant, only alluding to a most wonderful relationship on the personal level, is here now – the affirmation, the reality, and the culmination of it all. Jesus' death and Resurrection, all the healing power, all the Good News is focused down to each of us. Here in Baptism is the vastness of God's mercy and grace, His forgiveness and life, His partnership in life – all of this powerhouse is now plugged into our spiritual life. Christmas celebrates God come to share our lives, living among us at our level. Baptism simply continues the story, the message of the amazing love that God has for us, as Jesus shares *our* lives, living *in* us at our level. Even more, the Holy Spirit also lives in us, empowering us with faith, and is the Earnest/Guarantee of God's commitment.

St Mark apparently originally ends his Gospel [16:1-8] on a curious note:

168

After the Sabbath was past, Mary Magdalene, Mary the mother of James, and Salome bought spices, that they might come and anoint Him. Very early on the first day of the week, they came to the tomb, the sun having risen ... Entering the tomb, they saw a young man clothed in a white robe sitting on the right side; and they were astonished. But he said to them, "Do not be astonished; you seek Jesus of Nazareth, Who was crucified. He is risen! He is not here! See the place where they laid Him. But go, tell His disciples – and Peter – that He goes before you into Galilee; there you will see Him, as He told you."

So they went out quickly and fled from the tomb, for they trembled and were bewildered. They told no one anything, for they were afraid.

To end the Gospel this way seems very abrupt – so much so that the verses which follow are believed to be later additions meant to soften the ending and "finish" the story. It actually may be a mistake to add those verses. In fact, it is masterful for the ending to be left hanging: it forces the reader to finish the story for himself – how should it end? Should the story remain "in the tomb," or should the message indeed go out as the angel instructed and change people's lives? In fact, how did *we* find out if the witnesses to the Resurrection kept silent?

So also Baptism and this discussion must end like Mark's Gospel. The only ending is how the reader will "finish the story" for himself. Shall Baptism be "left in the tomb of doctrine," merely a collection of nice thoughts, but basically useless and incidental? Or will it be the growth of a relationship in which the reader becomes aware of all the lavish wealth of God available to him through this Sacrament? What meaning will it have for you?

10. Some Sermons

That We Should Be Called Children of God

> Behold what sort of Love the Father has bestowed upon us, that we should be called children of God – and we are! ... Beloved, we are now children of God; and it has not yet been revealed what we shall be, still we know that when He is revealed, we shall be like Him, for we shall see Him as He is.
>
> I John 3:1-2

A Melvin Hiscock once wrote in a *Reader's Digest* [no identification available other than page 120] about how, during his daughters' high school years, his family had adopted the slogan, "Remember who you are and what you stand for." Some time later, one daughter asked her boyfriend if it was OK if she went with a friend who was dateless for a party at his new job. He agreed, but added, "just remember *whose* you are and what *I'll* stand for."

"Behold what manner of love the Father has bestowed on us, that we should be called children of God" – for centuries up until recently, the second week after Easter was called "Misericordias Domini" or "the Mercy of God" Sunday, which came from the Introit or the Entrance Sentence of the day: "The land is filled with the mercy of the Lord." "Misericordias" is made up two words, "miseri" – "to pity" – and "cor" – "the heart" –, so it speaks of "heartfelt compassion" and so "mercy" is not a bad translation.

However this word entered into whole new class of meaning when the Bible was translated into Latin, when "misericordias" became the word of choice for the Old Testament Hebrew term "Hesed." "Hesed´ is one of those words that really cannot be translated very well, because when used of God, it attempts to plumb the depths of the heart of God, and there is just no word in any language that is adequate to *that* task. In English, "Hesed´ is translated as "steadfast love, mercy, kindness," and other terms that really do not quite do the job. In the New Testament Greek, its equally difficult counterpart, of which you may already be familiar, is "Agape" – that word for "love" which we see in the text I just read: "Behold what manner of *love* the Father has."

So if we were to think of the title of today, "Misericordias Domini" Sunday, the emphasis is as the Introit put it, "The land is filled with the Lord (the Creator of the Universe, the Jehovah of Covenant, the God of Glory)'s heartfelt, merciful, steadfast love." Indeed that is an ideal title for today, since that is exactly what we will see as we come to the Baptism of Alayna.

God's heartfelt, steadfast, merciful love – "Behold, what manner of love the Father has bestowed upon us, that we should be called children of God." Can you imagine how precious this identity is? It is something that should make us drop to our knees when we realize what it means to be actually be "God's children." Now please realize this in not the insipid idea that all creatures, or to narrow it down, that all humans are children of God. That popular belief does not even touch what John as well as St Paul are talking about when *they* use this phrase.

No, for their understanding we have to go back to Bethlehem and behold a human child in a manger in a stable. But this is not just any human child, for we discover that both God and Man are in one Person in this baby. God the Son has become a human, the Creator has stepped down to become His own creature. He is now subject to time and space. He is subject now to the health and welfare of His body. He is now subject to human emotions: He feels our griefs and our despairs, our joys and our amazements.

He does this in order to live our life, that life which we should have lived to please God, which we must live, which we cannot live because of the destructiveness of our sin [Hebrews 2:17]. *His* life was without blemish [I Peter 1:19] – He was faultless as was proclaimed by the prophecy of God [Isaiah 53:9], by the declaration of Pilate [Luke 23:4], even by the High Priest's false witnesses who could not make any charge stand against Him [Matthew 26:59-61]. Therefore the innocent Lamb of God lived in our place, died in our place – and then rose from the dead so that we could have an eternity, a life forever in the presence of the Father.

But there is another reason why He became human. Think of a suspension bridge – both ends have to be firmly anchored before anyone can go from one side to the other. That's one of the things that the Baby in Bethlehem has done: on one side He is firmly anchored in God because He is God the Son; and now, in that manger in that stable, the other side is firmly anchored in humanity. If Jesus had not become Man, then Baptism could never have made us become the children of God.

By Baptism we are placed on that Bridge called Jesus. In this act, Paul says we are buried with Jesus into death, so that like He was raised from death by the glory of the Father, *we also* have newness of life – actually, Paul even says "we shall certainly be united with Him in a resurrection like His" [Romans 6:4,5]. This is where it gets interesting, because if we are united with Him, then the other side of this Bridge, we discover, is that its anchor is not merely in heaven – it (or better, Jesus) is anchored *in God*. Why are we called the sons and daughters of God? It is because in Baptism, united to Jesus, we find ourselves on that end of the Bridge which is *the Son of God*.

We are not God's children in some romantic generalized all-creatures sense, nor are we "like Him" as if we become little gods ourselves, no, we are *in the Son of God* and therefore we participate in what He is, or as St Peter put it, we have become "partakers of the divine nature" [II,1:4] and through this we have become the children of God.

Now perhaps this all sounds like confusing mental gymnastics, but actually being "in Christ" is really quite an important concept in the Bible – in fact, that phrase is one of Paul's most favorite word images in his writings. Consider for the moment the kind of relationship that is going on constantly between the Father, the Son and the Holy Spirit. How could we ever describe the extraordinary heartfelt closeness between the Persons of the Trinity. There just is no way we can even begin to imagine the love, the fellowship and the communication that flows between them – just remember that problem we had earlier, trying to describe what "Hesed" and "Agape" mean!

Now remember, we are "in Jesus," we are in the middle of all of this flow of mutual love within the Godhead. Everything that Jesus receives from the Father flows right to us. This is what is behind what Paul says in Ephesians, chapter 2[:4-7] – and listen for the phrase "in Christ":

God, being rich in mercy, through His great Love with which He loved us, even us being dead in trespasses, <u>made us alive together *with Christ*</u> (by grace you are being saved) – and <u>raised us up together</u>, and <u>made us sit together in the heavenly places *in Christ Jesus*</u>, so that He might show in the coming ages the surpassing riches of His grace in kindness toward us *in Christ Jesus*.

Baptism is the beginning of what Jesus means when He said, "Abide in Me, and I in you" [John 14:4]. There in the God's impossible-to-understand relationship of love and closeness, in this atmosphere of "the immeasurable riches of His grace in His kindness" – there we are, right in its middle, right in its pathway, as it swirl around us. This intensity of His love gets even better when you remember that in Baptism, the Holy Spirit also comes to make His home in us, with one of the aims being that Father wants to hear the deep things of our own hearts, those things that we could never have put into words – just as much as the Father listens closely to the heart of His Son, so also He wants to *hear us*.

Baptism declares, that even though we have our moments where we feel separated, where God seems distant, where there just seems to be a black hole in the sky, that *that* is never the truth. "No!" this Sacrament declares: constantly circulating all around and through us the flow of love, care, involvement, grace and kindness that is internal to the nature of God – and because we are "in Christ," then there is no other choice, God is deeply involved with us. We have an unshakeable confidence.

With this background, now that little story with which I began plays its part. Baptism does not encourage us to remember "who we are" – because even as a child of God, our concepts of ourselves can be far too faulty, influenced by whatever mood or circumstance happens on this or that day. No, Baptism reminds us *"Whose* we are" – remember that Baptism is always passive: we *are Baptized*, we don't Baptize ourselves. God reaches down and takes Alayna, you, me and places us into Christ, on that Bridge, where we end up in God the Son, in the midst of a relationship that is impossible to find words for – all because that is *His* choice, *His* desire, *His* action – and *His* love.

What a wonderful security that gives to us! Think of when Jesus declared that even the hairs on our heads are all numbered [Matthew 10:30] – that is the intensity of God's interest in His Son, and we are right in the middle of that attention. Being so deeply imbedded into Christ fulfills the Psalmist's description [139], "where can I go from Your Spirit?" – heaven, death, east, west, dark, light, it does not matter. No wonder Jesus can say, "Lo, I am with you always" [Matthew 28:20], and "wherever two or three are gathered together in My Name, I am in their midst" [Matthew 18:20] – because not only is He in our midst, we are in His midst.

But there is also something else that is so wonderful about "Whose we are" – Luther reminds us that every time we turn to the Lord in repentance, we renew what happens in Baptism: we are again cleansed by Jesus "by the washing of Water in the Word, that He might present [us] to Himself, the Glorious Church, not having spot or wrinkle or any such thing, but that [we] should be holy and without blemish" [Ephesians 5:25-27]. Think of how every single time Jesus touches us with His forgiveness, all the old baggage, all the old burdens, all the pain and the distortion of life that sin brings with it is removed. In Jesus we stand in God, and we stand thoroughly clean, thoroughly delightful – as delightful as Jesus Himself is – to the Father.

This is what we are placing Alayna right into the middle of. What a wild ride of God's love is she in for! "Behold! – here at the font – "what manner of love the Father has given to that *we* should be called the Children of God – *and so we are!*"

Born of God

> For all who are born of God overcomes the world [*cosmos*], and this is
> the victory which overcomes the world – our faith   I John 5:4

In the television series "Dr. Quinn," the preacher once told a story that
really fits in well for today. A king came to a town and announced that he
had switched one of the children of the town with his own child, but he was
not going to tell which one was his. Then the king left.

The people were perplexed. They knew that they had better not treat the
royal child cruelly, lest the king come and destroy them. So they treated all
the children with dignity and respect. Many years later the king returned to a
much different town, a much happier one.

As he visited one older woman on her death bed, she whispered to the
king that she knew which child was of royal blood – her daughter. The king
replied that it was true, because all the children were his children.

The TV program had its own purpose for using this little story, but it is
one that fits well with one of today's theme. "As newborn babes..." begins
the Introit or Entrance Thought that was used for hundreds of years for this
first Sunday after the Resurrection. The foundation of this thought was this
Sunday's accent on Baptism and on the beginning of a person's walk in faith.
How much more fitting the opening anecdote is, when with the accent for
this Sunday we are reminded that in Baptism we are indeed *ALL* God's very
own children!

We need to stop every so often and realize again how very precious it is
to have the distinction of being a child of the royal Blood of the universe.
That's why the first Sunday following every major festival always has
something in its theme and lessons which accents Baptism, so that we might
have the opportunity to take another look at a most wonderful gift from God.

Do you realize that the privilege of beginning your prayers by calling
God your "Father" does not belong to you by nature? Just what gives you
the *right* to audaciously call the Creator of the whole universe your F*ather*?
God is just, righteous, perfect, and holy; He abhors evil; He requires total
perfection or else He sends judgment. He dwells in the majesty with the
angels, governing whole galaxies with countless planets, of which how many
are perhaps inhabited? And a tiny, minute speck in this vast universe has the
audacity to not only to call this God his Father, but to expect that this God
would even listen and respond to this speck's prayer – just what gives you
the right to expect that??

Some make a weak effort by quoting a popular phrase, "The Fatherhood of God, and the brotherhood of man," as if this should explain the right and the expectations that a human has in praying to God. But is this enough? Often the quoting of this phrase has behind it the idea that God has the moral obligation to listen to us, after all He created us, and therefore is responsible to sit on the edge of His great majestic heavenly throne, just waiting for us to tell Him what to do next.

Yet the people who quote this common phrase so often neatly forget to mention anything about how mankind has made it its business to run away from God; rejecting His ways and methods, rejecting His rules and commands – in fact, rejecting *Him*. Rarely do they account for God's reaction to the way that we have destroyed His creation; how we have created misery for ourselves and others, all the while blaming the problem on Him and others, and expecting Him to clean up the messes for us. How often have we slapped God in the face, spit upon Him and His Word by the way we act, speak, and think; and yet still expect God to fall all over Himself in His "moral" obligation to listen to and obey our requests?

In fact, the Bible says that we have gone so far in sin that all mankind has switched fathers. "You are of your father the Devil, and you desire to do your father's desires[lusts]," [John 8:44] Jesus told the Jews who refused to believe in Him; "You, being dead in trespasses and your sins in which you once walked..., according to the ruler of the power of the air, the spirit who is now at work in the sons of disobedience, ... and were by nature children of wrath just as the rest of mankind is" [Ephesians 2:1-3], St Paul tells the Ephesians. Suddenly, according the Bible's definition of who qualifies as the children of God, we find ourselves having no right to expect anything from God, much less that we would expect to be called His children.

At this point, easily our prayers could either cease or else merely become empty exercises, vague movements of air, vain attempts at psychological self-reassurance, accomplishing basically nothing.

It is against this backdrop that the Good News of Good Friday, Easter, and Baptism come as such a powerful comfort and hope. These important events make God step far beyond merely being a groundskeeper of the earth and its inhabitants. Rather they make us vividly aware of just how God has so earnestly desired to raise US up to an astounding position of importance and value to this Creator and Ruler of this vast universe.

Baptism has such an amazing message! But first is to realize that it is not some kind of magic, by which we gain control over God, instead it is God invading the orphanage of our spiritual lives, coming upon a rebellious child such as we can be, and then going before the *cosmos* [world] to declare that He wants us – not just for the time being, but literally forever. The enormous impact of this thought comes across clearly when we realize that we Baptize, not because it is a nice thing to do, but because we are under *command* – we are under the direct order of Jesus. We have no choice, because this is what *God* wants to do – *He wants to declare us as His children.*

What an astounding thing, when God demands that we do this very, very simple thing, just so that He can stoop to this tiny little speck in all the universe, and proclaim to a universe that this speck is now His *child*, whom He wants by His side forever, whom He will listen to for his every word, and whom He will watch over with the same zealous care as when a parent watches over his only child. The scenario becomes even more amazing when we realize that for this to happen meant that this God would first have to give His only Son to death for this little speck. It is enough to make you stagger in amazement!

And that brings out something else which is special about Baptism. This relationship that we are set into has an added dimension. We do not merely become God's children. According to the Word of God, we are not merely placed into a family alongside millions of other children. We are placed into the position of being the only Child of God – because God has declared that in Baptism we are placed into Christ, into Jesus. Can you possibly imagine the relationship that Jesus has with the Father? Can you possibly describe the mutual love and intensive listening that must go on between these to Persons within the Godhead of the Trinity? And then to realize that you are right in the very middle of that relationship! Think of the tremendous singular love that must be shared between the Father and the Son – and you are in the middle of it!

You are right in the middle of all that Jesus is and has – what a tremendous wealth of resources literally surround you, as you are plunged deep into Jesus and all that He is! And if all this surrounding you weren't enough, the Holy Spirit comes to live within you – you actually carry God around in you! There just is no way to describe how you, a mere speck in the *cosmos*, suddenly would have such one-on-one, personal, individual, deep communion with Ruler of the vast universe.

Yet, how often we treat this relationship with God with utmost casualness! Parents talk about having their children "done" as if this were merely some sort of cake in the oven. Or else there is little or no effort to share with their child the wonder, the hope, the depth of what this very special relationship describes.

But perhaps the worst is when we do have an idea of the tremendous importance and value that God places on this singular event and what it accomplishes, that we treat it as of minor significance to our own selves. How often do we live with stooped shoulders and heads bowed by the cares and worries of life, rather than to hold our heads up, and with hope and confidence and strength live like the very special people we are! How often can it seem that we are intent on living as anything other than the royalty of the universe, a child of God Himself! In our actions, our words, our thoughts do we live as a people who dwell in the middle of an amazing and indescribable relationship between God the Father and God the Son?

To our shame we treat this precious gift of Baptism as such a minor and casual thing! And yet the Lord comes back to us time and again with graciousness and love, in which He patiently forgives yet another time of our foolishness, and makes us realize all over again the tremendous gift He has given us. Isn't that why we celebrate Christmas, Good Friday, Easter, Baptism, and all the other major festivals every single year?! because these occasions reflect the depth of the forgiveness of the Ruler of this vast universe, and His utmost patience with you and me, His beloved and highly honored children.

This is the whole secret for the profound confidence that St John can have when He states in the text for this morning that whatever is born of God overcomes the world – because John constantly emphasizes this wonderful position that we hold because of Baptism – we ARE the children of God. And when you think of it, what a victory that is!

Come this morning and celebrate again, the wonderful gift that God has given to each of us, through that very, very simple, yet very, very profound gift of Baptism.

Endnotes

[1] Some of this material is from James Lindemann, *Covenant: The Blood is the Life*. (Lethbridge, Alberta: RFLindemann & Son, 2011), 17-19 – ISBN: paper - 978-0-9877280-0-5; epub - 978-0-9877280-4-3; pdf - 978-0-9877280-7-4; a self-published book, see author's website at www.lindespirit.com for acquiring.

[2] H. Clay Trumbull, *The Blood Covenant: A Primitive Rite and Its Bearing on Scripture* (Reprint Publisher: Kirkwood, Mo.: Impact Christian Books, 1975), 38.

[3] Walter R. Roehrs, "Divine Covenants: Their Structure and Function," Concordia Journal (Concordia Publishing House, St. Louis, Mo) 1/1988, 12.

[4] "The soul of Jonathan was knit to the soul of David," and "for the life/soul of all flesh is its Blood" [Leviticus 17:14], therefore it is no surprise that Covenant would define what has already occurred.

[5] Berthold von Schenk, *The Presence* (New York: Ernst Kaufman, Inc., 1945), 41.

[6] Richard Lovelace, Dynamics of Spiritual Life (Downers Grove: InterVarsity Press, 1979), p. 89.

[7] Circumcision was 1 year old when Isaac was circumcised on the eighth day,
Isaac was 60 at the birth of Jacob (Genesis 25:26);
Jacob was 130 upon entering Egypt (Genesis 47:9);
Israel would be "enslaved and mistreated four hundred years" in Egypt (Genesis 15:13; Acts 7:6)
= just shy of 600 years.
Gal 3:16-17 seems to indicate 430 years from Abraham whereas Exodus 12:40-41 speaks of 430 years in Egypt (which probably included Joseph's thirty years).

[8] Every Roman soldier knew that he must be dead before the seal is broken.

[9] See Matthew 18:16; John 8:17; II Corinthians 13:1; Hebrews 10:28.

[10] Lindemann, *Covenant*, 343, 347-8

[11] *Theological Dictionary of the New Testament* [TDNT], ed by Gerhard Kittel, trans. and ed by Geoffrey W. Bromiley, Vol I (Wm. B. Eerdmans Publishing Company: Grand Rapids, Mich), 1968), 539-540

[12] Paul E. Billheimer, "Destined For The Throne" (Christian Literature Crusade: Fort Washington, Penn, 1976), pp 33,35-37.

[13] Theodore H. Epp, *Praying With Authority*, Back to the Bible Broadcast (1965), 70-71

[14] Robert F Lindemann, "Reflections Upon Holy Baptism," unpublished paper.

[15] See James Lindemann, *Celebration – Holy Communion: A Love Story* (Lethbridge, Alberta: RFLindemann & Son, 2012) – ISBN: paper - 978-0-9916866-0-5; epub - 978-0-9916866-1-2; pdf - 978-0-9916866-2-9; a self-published book, see author's website at www.lindespirit.com for acquiring.

[16] Francis E. Reinberger, *How to Pray*, Fortress Press (1964), 18-19.

[17] Martin Luther, "The Adoration of the Sacrament" *Luther's Works (American Edition), Volume 36: Word and Sacrament II* (General Editors: Jaroslav Pelikan and Helmut T. Lehmann; Mulenberg Press: Philadelphia, 1960), 302.

[18] Although translated as "now" or "at last," the Hebrew word carries more of the idea of a one-time occurrence.

[19] See pages 146-147.

[20] Don Fortner, "Cannot Sin," Grace Baptist Church Danville, Ky. http://www.sovereign-grace.com/2366a.htm.

[21] Martin Luther, *Small Catechism.*

[22] Neil T. Anderson "Do Christians Still Have a Sin Nature?", (adapted from: Dr. Robert Saucy and Dr. Neil T. Anderson *God's Power at Work in You*, Harvest House].

[23] Lindemann, *Celebration!*, 31.

[24] Martin Luther, "The Treatise on the New Testament, that is, the Holy Mass" (1520), *Luther's Works (American Edition), Volume 35: Word and Sacrament I* (General Editors: Jaroslav Pelikan and Helmut T. Lehmann: Mulenberg Press: Philadelphia, 1960), 82.

[25] Andrew Das, "Baptism in the New Testament", website: http://www.mtio.com/articles/aissar84.htm, retrieved 2012-12-08.

[26] Martin Luther, "The Babylonian Captivity of the Church" *Luther's Works (American Edition), Volume 36: Word and Sacrament II* (General Editors: Jaroslav Pelikan and Helmut T. Lehmann: Mulenberg Press: Philadelphia, 1960), 62

[27] From an unpublished sermon by the author on 2005-09-12.

[28] Von Schenk, 31-32.

[29] Martin Luther, "The Sacrament of Penance" (1519), *Luther's Works (American Edition), Volume 35 Word and Sacrament I* (General Editors: Jaroslav Pelikan and Helmut T. Lehmann: Mulenberg Press: Philadelphia, 1960), 19.

[30] Bob Deffinbaugh, "The High Priestly Prayer of Jesus (John 17)," http://www.bible.org/page.asp?page_id=625.

[31] Rev. John Scott Johnson, "In Defense of Infant Baptism," http://www.mountainretreatorg.net/apologetics/baptism3.html:

> The proof text for this objection is Mark 16:16: "He that believeth and is baptized, shall be saved; but he that believeth not, shall be damned."
>
> If the first part of the verse excludes infant baptism, because infants cannot believe, the second part denies infant salvation for the same reason. ... But why interpret one half of a verse one way and refuse to take the other half the same way?

[32] Robert F. Lindemann, unpublished paper.

[33] Francis A. Schaeffer, "Baptism," http://www.spiritone.com/~wing/fs_bapt.htm.

Also McMahon, "My Retraction":

> I should have said it like this: the Apostles had no need of a positive sanction in order to continue the inclusion of infants in the covenant because they have always been

included in every covenant through the history of redemption. This is a different statement altogether and does not allow for looking up baptism Scriptures in the New Testament as a remedy or answer to the question of Infant Baptism... Furthermore, there is not one "reference" to Infant Baptism in the New Testament. The Baptist argues that the reason for this is because Jesus or the Apostles did not teach it. The Paedo-Baptist argues that the Jews had a very good idea of infant inclusion in the covenant since every covenant and every dealing with those infants of believing households up until this time did include infants. They would not have needed another lesson on that again – their lessons concerning covenant theology have lasted as long as men have walked the earth... Instead, what we find is the New Testament, everywhere, mentioning covenant theology in terms like "households." This is very strange language for the Baptist to deal with since "household" is a covenant term the Jews would have certainly understood, and the New Testament church would have required, as Jews, entire households to become part of the church. This is not Baptist Theology at all. In fact, of all the treatises I have read on Baptistic theology in this area, none make good mention, or any at all, on why the term "household" is even used by the Holy Sprit all through the book of Acts if "individualism" (single converts coming to faith apart from familial relations) is now the norm (especially with the Greek forms surrounding this word).

[34] This section is from the author's book, *Covenant: The Blood is the Life.*

[35] Martin Luther, "That These Words of Christ, 'This Is My Body,' etc., Still Stand Firm Against the Fanatics" (1527), in *Luther's Works*, Vol 37 (*Word and Sacrament III*), gen. ed. Helmut T. Lehmann, (Philadelphia: Muhlenberg Press, 1960), 127.

[36] Das, "Baptism":

> When the Gentiles receive the Spirit, Peter concludes before his Jerusalem audience that who was he to "hinder" (koluein) God. Peter uses the same word "hinder" (koluein) in Acts 11[:17] that he had used in Acts 10:47 in relation to the need for the people to be baptized. Even as no one should hinder baptism, so Peter says that he must not hinder God. To hinder the people from being baptized is to HINDER GOD. It is GOD who is at work in baptism.

[37] Dr Martin H Scharlemann, *The Secret of God's Plan: Studies in Ephesians,* (Saint Louis, Missouri: Concordia Publishing House, 1970), 20.

[38] Theodore H. Epp, "Praying With Authority," Back to the Bible Broadcast (1965), 69-70.

[39] Billheimer, 89.

[40] The Church of Jesus Christ of the Latter-Day Saints (Mormon)'s version is that this would be "the Holy Spirit," a difficult to define substance, which is distinct from "the Holy Ghost." "The Holy Ghost" is a person who has attained godship, but who has originally been formed from "the Holy Spirit" in the same way as all people are.

[41] Charles Spurgeon.

[42] Martin Luther, "The Blessed Sacrament of the Holy and True Body of Christ, and the Brotherhoods," *Luther's Works (American Edition), Volume 35: Word and Sacrament I,* General Editors: Jaroslav Pelikan and Helmut T. Lehmann (Philadelphia: Mulenberg

Press, 1960), 54, 57; although this is in regard to Holy Communion, the message is the same.

[43] Walter J. Burghardt, "Come, Lord Jesus!", *Marriage* Magazine, 12/74, 3.

[44] Luther, "Babylonian," 73.

[45] Martin Luther, *Large Catechism*, Project Gutenberg, retrieved 2005-02-02.

[46] Apparently in the decades after World War II, the arrogance of United States tourists left many in foreign lands with a very bad opinion of the country as a whole.

[47] Lora Lee Parrott, *Meals from the Manse Cook Book* quoted in *Speakers Book of Illustrative Stories,* ed by Maxwell Droke (Droke House, Indianapolis: 1956), 110.

[48] Lindemann, *Celebration*, 124.

[49] Andrew Murray, *With Christ in the School of Prayer*.

[50] Martin Luther, "A Treatise... the Holy Mass," 99.

[51] Andrew Murray, *With Christ in the School of Prayer*, website: http://www.worldinvisible.com/library/murray/5bm.10353/5bm.10353.c.htm.

[52] What is happening in this little interchange between pastor and congregation? The pastor blesses the people ("The Lord be with you!") and then, in return, *the people bless him* – especially "with your *spirit!*" which is the area of the pastor's dual function as spokesman for God and spokesman for the people. This interchange often occurs in past liturgies before three significant actions: when the pastor "collects" the thought of the day in prayer; when he consecrates and distributes Holy Communion; and when he pronounces the benediction, the final blessing of the Liturgy.

[53] Murray, *School of Prayer*.

[54] "An Unknown Christian," *The Kneeling Christian,* Zondervan Publishing House (1966), 60.

[55] Martin Luther "Receiving Both Kinds in the Sacrament" *Luther's Works (American Edition), Volume 36: Word and Sacrament II* (General Editors: Jaroslav Pelikan and Helmut T. Lehmann: Mulenberg Press: Philadelphia), 245.

[56] *Theological Dictionary of the New Testament (TDNT)*, ed by Gerhard Kittel, trans. and ed by Geoffrey W. Bromiley, Vol I (Wm. B. Eerdmans Publishing Company: Grand Rapids, Mich), 1968) Vol I, p 536.

[57] Supplementary Volume of *The Interpreter's Dictionary of the Bible*, p 87.

[58] See website: http://www.earlychristianwritings.com/didache.html.

[59] Lindemann, *Covenant,* 50.

[60] Edmund Schlink, *The Doctrine Of Baptism*, ed by Herbert JA Bouman (CPH: St Louis, 1972), pp 127-28.

[61] Robert Lindemann, unpublished paper: "Reflections Upon Holy Baptism", 4.

[62] *TDNT*, ed by Gerhard Kittel, vol I, p 540.

[63] Some of this material is from Lindemann, *Covenant, 17-19.*

[64] *Numbers,* in *The Pulpit Commentary,* ed. H.D.M. Spence and Joseph S. Exell, (NY, NY: Funk & Wagnalls Company, 1950), 240.

[65] Note Hebrews 9:13-14:

> For if the Blood of bulls and goats and the ashes of a heifer, sprinkling the unclean, sanctifies for the purifying of the flesh, how much more shall the Blood of Christ, Who through the eternal Spirit offered Himself without spot to God, cleanse your conscience from dead works to serve the living God?

[66] Gary D. Practico and Miles V VanPelt, *Basics of Biblical Hebrew, Chapter 4 b,* http://blakleycreative.com/jtb/BBH/BBH_OH_04.pdf, retrieved 2013-02-03.

[67] Das, "Baptism."

[68] Ibid.

[69] Richard Jungkuntz, *Gospel of Baptism* (Saint Louis, Mo: Concordia Publishing House, 1968), p 111,118-19.